Critical Issues in Peace and Education

Routledge Research in Education

For a full list of titles in this series, please visit www.routledge.com

Critical Issues in Peace and Education

Edited by
Peter Pericles Trifonas
and Bryan Wright

Routledge
Taylor & Francis Group

NEW YORK AND LONDON

First published 2011
by Routledge
2 Park Square, Milton Park, Abingdon, Oxon OX14 4RN

Simultaneously published in the USA and Canada
by Routledge
711 Third Avenue, New York, NY10017

Routledge is an imprint of the Taylor & Francis Group, an informa business

First issued in paperback 2014

The right of Peter Pericles Trifonas and Bryan Wright to be identified as the authors of the editorial material, and of the authors for their individual chapters, has been asserted by them in accordance with sections 77 and 78 of the Copyright, Designs and Patents Act 1988.

Typeset in Sabon by Taylor & Francis Books

Library of Congress Cataloging-in-Publication Data
Critical issues in peace and education / edited by Peter Pericles Trifonas and Bryan Wright.
p. cm. -- (Routledge research in education; 42)
Includes bibliographical references and index.
1. Peace--Study and teaching. 2. Human rights--Study and teaching.
3. Education, Humanistic. 4. Multicultural education. I. Trifonas, Peter Pericles, 1960- II. Wright, Bryan.
JZ5534.C75 2010
303.6'6071--dc22
2010010127

ISBN13: 978-0-415-87368-0 (hbk)
ISBN13: 978-1-138-02183-9 (pbk)
ISBN13: 978-0-203-84485-4 (ebk)

Contents

To Caroline Lauder,
We shall find peace. We shall hear angels. We shall see the sky sparkling with diamonds.

PT

My heartfelt thanks and deep appreciation to fellow scholars and friends that have challenged the boundaries of thought concerning peace and education

Bryan Wright

Contributors

Michael W. Apple is John Bascom Professor of Curriculum and Instruction and Educational Policy Studies at the University of Wisconsin, Madison. He has written extensively on the relationship among knowledge, power, and educational reform. Among his recent books are Educating the "Right" Way (2nd edn., 2006), The Subaltern Speak (2006), and The Routledge International Handbook of Critical Education (2009).

Kathy Bickmore is Associate Professor and Coordinator of the Graduate Program in Curriculum at the Ontario Institute for Studies in Education, University of Toronto, Canada. She teaches (graduate and teacher education) and conducts research about education for constructive conflict, peacebuilding, conflict resolution, equity, and citizenship/democratization in public school contexts. Her work has appeared in books such as Handbook of Conflict Management and How Children Understand War and Peace, and journals such as Conflict Resolution Quarterly, Theory and Research in Social Education, Curriculum Inquiry, Alberta Journal for Educational Research, and Theory Into Practice. Recent publications include guest editing the theme issue of Theory and Research in Social Education (32:1, Winter 2004), "Education for Peacebuilding Citizenship."

Mario Di Paolantonio is Assistant Professor at York University, Toronto, Canada. His research explores the pedagogical implications of artistic memorial practices that arise as an effect or response to state-sanctioned initiatives to come to terms with historical wrongs. He is an International Research Associate with the Unit for Global Justice at Goldsmiths College, University of London, and at the Centro de Estudios en Pedagogías Contemporáneas (CEPEC), Escuela de Humanidades (EHU) at the Universidad Nacional de San Martín (UNSAM), Buenos Aires, Argentina.

Grace Feuerverger is a professor at the Ontario Institute for Studies in Education (OISE) of the University of Toronto. Her research interests focus on theoretical and practical issues of cultural and linguistic diversity, ethnic identity maintenance, and minority language learning within multicultural educational contexts, as well as on conflict resolution and peacemaking in international settings. Her award-winning book Oasis of Dreams: Teaching and Learning Peace in a Jewish-Palestinian Village in Israel (New York and London: RoutledgeFalmer, 2001) is a reflexive ethnography based on a nine-year study Feuerverger carried out as researcher in an extraordinary cooperative Jewish-Arab village in Israel and it has become an international role model for a pedagogy of peace. Her new book Teaching, Learning and Other Miracles (Rotterdam: Sense Publishers, 2007) explores teaching and learning in schools as a sacred life journey, a quest toward liberation. In an era of narrow agendas of "efficiency" and "control," this book dares to suggest that education is and should always be about uplifting the human spirit.

Ilan Gur-Ze'ev is a professor and philosopher of education at the University of Haifa. He is an involved intellectual with an academic interest in peace education; critical theory; critical pedagogy; postcolonialism, feminism, multiculturalism, Holocaust education, Higher Education and philosophy. His books have been published in Hebrew, Portuguese, Arabic, Flemish, German, English, Polish, Slovak and the Flemish language.

Magnus Haavelsrud is Professor of Education at the Norwegian University of Science and Technology in Trondheim, Norway. His work deals with the critique of the reproductive role of education and the possibilities of transcendence of this reproduction in light of the traditions of educational sociology and peace research. He took part in the creation of the Peace Education Commission of the International Peace Research Association at the beginning of the 1970s and served as the Commission's second Executive Secretary, 1975–79. He was the Program Chair for the World Conference on Education in 1974 and edited the proceeding from this conference entitled Education for Peace: Reflection and Action. He served as the Carl-von-Ossietzky Guest Professor of the German Council for Peace and Conflict Research. His publications include Education in Developments (1996), Perspektiv i utdannings-sosiologi (Perspectives in the Sociology of Education) (2nd edn., 1997), Education Within the Archipelago of Peace Research 1945–64 (co-authored with Mario Borrelli, 1993), Disarming: Discourse on Violence and Peace (1993), and Approaching Disarmament Education (1981).

Maria Hantzopoulos is Assistant Professor of Education at Vassar College in Poughkeepsie, New York. She also taught social studies for many years at Humanities Preparatory Academy, an award-winning small public high school in New York City. She has worked with organizations such as the Coalition of Essential Schools, ASPIRA of New York, and Global Kids and has worked locally and internationally with youth on human rights and peace education initiatives. She remains active in local educational reform issues, including matters pertaining to high-stakes testing, new small school development, the school-to-prison pipeline and restorative justice practices for and with youth.

Brian W. Lagotte is a PhD candidate and lecturer at the University of Wisconsin-Madison. His work combines Anthropology and Education Policy to examine how knowledge about policy is created, manipulated, and interpreted by those affected. His other projects include historical studies of Japanese educational reform and exploring the interaction between law, policy, and society.

Peter Pericles Trifonas is a professor at the Ontario Institute for Studies in Education/University of Toronto. His areas of interest include ethics, philosophy of education, cultural studies, and technology. Among his books are the following: Revolutionary Pedagogies: Cultural Politics, Instituting Education, and the Discourse of Theory (Routledge, 2000), The Ethics of Writing: Derrida, Deconstruction, and Pedagogy (Rowman & Littlefield, 2000), The Right to Philosophy (with Jacques Derrida), Roland Barthes and the Empire of Signs (Icon, 2001), Umberto Eco and Football (Icon, 2001), and Pedagogies of Difference (Routledge, 2003).

Bryan Wright is a PhD Candidate in Curriculum, Teaching, and Learning with a specialization in the Philosophy of Peace Education at the Ontario Institute for Studies in Education/University of Toronto. Additionally, he is an Adjunct Professor in the Graduate Program in Conflict Resolution at Portland State University, Portland, Oregon. His research interests center on the development of grounded philosophies for peace and education within the Western academy. Some of his other research and teaching interests include social justice education, collaborative pedagogy, transformative education, and education/curricular research on peace. His Master's thesis, Educating for Cultures of Peace within the Academy was published by VDM Verlag Dr. Müller, Saarbrücken, Germany.

Introduction

Peter Pericles Trifonas and Bryan Wright

Peace and peace education have been seen as suspect concepts within the academy, given their trope and historical baggage throughout the ages. The varied emphases of peace education, as propounded by individual scholars, have served a heuristic function for attempts to found the basis of a discipline for thought and action, while being strongly driven by both the cultural and national settings in which the field has begun to germinate theory and practice. It has been difficult to define peace education succinctly, let alone reach an undisputed consensus on a definition of peace, yet many adept researchers and scholars have offered excellent concepts to build upon (Reardon, 1988, 1999, 2001; Harris and Morrison, 2003). One common conceptualization of peace may be "the absence of violence to any aspect of human life" (Anderson, 1985). Consensus on common definitions of peace, culture, and peace education has been difficult at best, as individual body politics—such as nation-states—have prescribed definitions and usage of both terms in their own interest over the centuries. However, many prominent peace researchers across the world have sought to bridge the socio-political divide offering similar conceptualizations of peace education based on a more holistic approach (Reardon, 1999; Gur-Ze'ev, 2001; Harris and Morrison, 2003) that would enfold the values of diversity in subjectivity as articulated and promulgated by the communities of difference represented across the pedagogies of feminist, critical, anti-racist or postcolonial, and gay and lesbian theories. This holistic movement for peace education, rooted in human dignity, is beginning to take shape though it still remains largely unformed (Harris, 2004; Salomon, 2006). It has indeed been informed by the attempts of these pedagogical movements to break down and reconceptualize the normative basis of subjectivity that has been operationalized in strictly ethical terms by the Western conventions of schooling systems as a manifest curricular goal or outcome (Apple, 1990; Derrida, 1990; Trifonas, 2000b).

Educational institutions have traditionally not questioned subjective differences among student populations and have been loathe to examine the role of peace in respective societies while disavowing the performative role in peace with which they are charged. Peace education would approach this reticence in a deliberate transdisciplinary perspective that fully acknowledges the subjectivity of difference in place, space, and time while pursuing the human dignity of all persons with absolute equanimity. The concept of disciplinarity is becoming one of the major hurdles in peace studies in general and peace education specifically. Disciplinarity, as it has been constructed and construed within the academy, has posed a significant challenge to peace, given the territoriality, implied provenience, and rigidity of both disciplines and fields. Peace studies in general, and peace education specifically should be built on a trans-disciplinary model as multi-, inter-, and cross-disciplinary approaches are inadequate to the task of the encompassing nature of peace and conflict (Galtung, 2004). Johan Galtung's suggestion of drawing on the "tool chests of several disciplines" (ibid.), such as the medical model, affords a more holistic approach to understanding and enlightens the conversation around many epistemological questions. Leading advocates of transdisciplinarity acknowledge its complementarity with more traditional disciplinary approaches offering a visionary joining in dialogue of the "exact sciences ... with the humanities and the social sciences, as well as with art, literature, poetry, and spiritual experience" (de Freitas et al., 1994). Transdisciplinarity informed by pedagogies formed around the critical issues of peace and education can then be understood as the reformation of education and thought as it "concerns that which is at once between the disciplines, across the different disciplines, and beyond all discipline." Its goal is the understanding of the present world, of which one imperative is the unity of which demonstrates the indisputable relation between peace and transdisciplinarity. Opening the links among disciplines in an examination of the discursive formations of the theories of knowledge continues the spirit of curricular reconceptualization and progressive education that originally began with the social reconstructionist movement of the 1920s and is notably present today in the form of feminist pedagogies, critical pedagogies, anti-racist or postcolonial pedagogies, and gay pedagogies (Dewey, 1916; Trifonas, 2000b).

The archeology of knowledge and its institutionalization are highly contested in these maturing pedagogies that challenge the fundamental construction of the Western paradigm, its educational institutions, and its reproductive nature. But the continuum of educational reform marked by the days of John Dewey and his contemporaries, to include the recognition of the values of difference as a legitimate and integral feature of a modern civil society, has critically shifted to an explicit recognition of such difference encompassed within an emerging sense of community within a closed ecosystem. An explicit recognition of difference as propounded through a transdisciplinary conceptualization of peace education would integrate ways of knowing, being, and learning to facilitate a broader perspective for a critical discussion of the issues that embroil us in questions of social justice and peace. Critical Issues in Peace and Education asks theorists and educational practitioners from around the globe to reflect upon the possibilities of articulating a "curriculum of difference" for peace that critically examines the cross-cultural issues of peace and education in relation to questions of culture, identity, and meaning that are at the forefront of global education issues today.

In Chapter 1, "Educational Reform and the Project of Militarization," Brian Lagotte and Michael Apple analyze how economic pressures generated by neoliberalism, mixed with foreign policy adventures driven by neoconservatives, have increasingly affected education reform in disturbing ways. This chapter situates the most important American federal education policy, the No Child Left Behind Act (NCLB), in this larger context. Further, it highlights how militarization is embedded in the policy and the various forms this takes on the ground in, and around, schools. As others in this volume speak in powerful ways about the possibility of education to promote peace, this chapter may serve to magnify the current consequences of taking this issue too lightly. The chapter is grounded in the controversies surrounding one of the more important but lesser-known parts of NCLB, Section 9528. This section is the gateway for the military to intervene in public high schools, either by gaining access to campuses or students' private directory information. The consequences of this policy, however, radiate outwards. First, the balance of visits by military recruiters or college recruiters can often can be mapped by examining the demographics and economic level of high schools. Second, the private sector has been tapped to fulfill data collection work to mask the Defense Department's denial that it is involved in database building. Finally, the chapter examines locations of contestation where parents, students, and local activist groups are resisting this encroachment on education by the armed forces.

In Chapter 2, "Encountering Peace: The Politics of Participation When Educating for Co-Existence," Maria Hanztopoulos maintains that the core and fundamental notion of dialogue in peace education and conflict resolution programs is often a taken-for-granted method; one that is an unsaid means for equalizing relationships, humanizing the "Other," and moving towards an ideal state of peace and understanding among "conflicting" groups. Drawing from and informed by practical experience, post-structural and feminist theories, and participant interviews, this chapter reflects upon, troubles, and offers a re-reading of key concepts such as dialogue and peace in such types of programs, raising questions about the assumptions embedded within these concepts, particularly how they are defined, embodied, manifest, performed, and experienced, by whom and for what reason(s). It explores the normative and commonsense qualities that are inherent in these concepts to shed light on possible ways they operate to monitor, subjugate, and control behaviors and ways of being and thinking. Finally, this chapter will examine how these programs can ignore existing asymmetrical power relations among groups, and considers the possibilities of less contrived spaces as potential sites for more authentic engagement.

Chapter 3, "A Grassroots Peace Education Innovation in a Co-operative Jewish-Palestinian Village in Israel: Mahatma Gandhi's Concept of 'Satyagraha' in Action" is based on a nine-year study that Grace Feuerverger carried out as ethnographer in an extraordinary village and it is about hope in the midst of deadly conflict. Neve Shalom/Wahat Al-Salam (the Hebrew and Arabic words for "Oasis of Peace") is an Israeli village that began as an intercultural experiment. There, Jews and Arabs founded a community aimed at demonstrating the possibilities of living in peace—while maintaining their respective cultural heritages and languages. Their daily search for a better world is both overwhelming and fascinating. From her own perspective as a child of Holocaust survivors, Feuerverger explores the woundings and sense of victimhood that both Israeli Jews and Palestinians feel in their very different ways. She shares narrative portraits of some remarkable educators who are working together in an everyday journey toward reconciliation and peaceful co-existence. Feuerverger offers insights into the extraordinary landscape of this co-operative village with its cultural encounters, educational innovations, moral dilemmas, negotiations and reconciliations, which form the basis for creating the vibrant spirit of this community against all odds.

In Chapter 4, "Learning Human Rights Praxis," Magnus Haavelsrud reflects on how education can contribute to the potential of the human being for becoming a protector and not a violator of human rights. This potential, he believes, is, at least to some extent, conditioned by the quality of learning experiences. This quality is again conditioned by the educator's comprehension of the field of human rights and which assumptions are made about the basic qualities of the human being and how these qualities may work for or against human rights development. Haavelsrud argues that the educator needs to develop an understanding of human rights in relation to other issues such as development and disarmament. It is also argued that the manifestation of human rights violations as well as human rights practices in the learner's everyday context is recognized and included as valid human rights knowledge. It follows that a dialogical communication form in human rights education is necessary in order to enable the learner to voice his/her observations of human rights violations and practices. Such learning experiences would open spaces for the learners to actively contribute in a praxis which involves transformation towards more human rights practices in the context in which the learner is situated. This kind of educational experience aims at recognizing the learner as a subject whose historical role it is to transform the world when problems and challenges are met. One condition for an education, which provides the learner with this kind of human rights education, is the professional formation of teachers. Teacher education is therefore an important venue for planning and implementing learning experiences in support of the socialization of the human being to become a human rights protector and practitioner.

In Chapter 5, "On Human Rights, Philosophy, and Education: The Ethics of Difference after Deconstruction," Peter Pericles Trifonas engages the ethical ground of difference for peace, philosophy, and education. The chapter presents a reading of the ethics of deconstruction and its incursion into the logic of the cosmopolitical that broaches the question of human rights, peace, and education. It is a moment of questioning directly addressing the academic responsibility of educational institutions and by extension those who teach, work, and live in them, and, perhaps, for them, as this is how the teaching body (le corps enseignant) begins and where it ends. What does this mean exactly? To say that a pedagogical institution, and those who are a part of it, are it, and possess total and unabiding and hence irresponsible and unaccountable control of the intellectual domain they survey is to surmise a legacy of exclusion. There is no space left to welcome another. It is a question of affinity and openness toward embracing the difference of the Other without giving way to hesitance or reservation, empirical qualification and moral judgment, let alone indignation. Trifonas contests that the question of a "proper domain" of the question of human rights, of institutions, of philosophy—of propriety and domination, appropriation, expropriation, of property, participation, ownership and fairness, and therefore of law, ethics, and ultimately, of social justice—brings us back to the connections between culture and knowledge.

In Chapter 6, "Education for 'Peace' in Urban Canadian Schools: Gender, Culture, Conflict, and Opportunities to Learn," Kathy Bickmore concludes that life revolves around conflicts and identities. Disagreements, problems, decisions, injustices, clashing perspectives or interests need negotiation and resolution for peace. Violence can be a symptom of underlying conflicts, and a way of handling conflicts, but it is not inevitable in all cases. The nonviolent confrontation of such conflicts is what sustains both democratic civil society and human relationships. Conflict can be explosive. Bickmore makes the case that typical urban public schools in Canada today do not embrace such conflicts as opportunities for learning and collectively creating dynamic peace. On the contrary, despite many notable shining exceptions, these schools seem much more often to ignore or actively repress expressions of difference in both implicit and explicit curriculum, focusing their efforts on achieving negative peace through control and conformity. It is a huge challenge that any peace education effort in public schools must operate in the context of this hegemonic patriarchal structure, while possibly trying to transform it from within.

In Chapter 7, "Improvisation, Violence, and Peace Education," Ilan Gur-Ze'ev explores how peace education is currently working hard to achieve homogeneity and ethnocentristic-oriented togetherness in the face of a growing awareness of the philosophical challenges presented by post-structuralist philosophies. This awareness, however, has not yet culminated in systematic reflection on the central challenges, conceptions, and aims of peace education, neither on its cultural, political, and philosophical pre-conditions, histories, and fruits. The chapter is aimed at contributing to this much-needed theoretical effort. Gur-Ze'ev maintains that peace education did not make the slightest effort to reconstruct its history, let alone a critical history of peace education as a spiritual, educational, and political effort that begins with the prophets and the early church and included various "heretic" movements and oppositions to the hegemonic theology, culture, and social structures. This chapter restricts itself to the aim of offering a short reflection on the relations between three concepts: peace, violence, and improvisation. It shows that the concept of improvisation might be of special relevance to any attempt to articulate and actualize counter-education which addresses the threats inflicted by the present-day peace education to free, anti-dogmatic, creative, and erotic humans.

In Chapter 8, "Deconstructing the Other: Opening Peace," Bryan Wright looks at the critical issues of peace and education in the university setting through a deconstructive lens that would strive to hold the Other in fundamental alterity in the realm of the cosmopolitical, which would imag(in)e the possibility of peace through the eyes of the Other. While this task seems quite daunting, and even impossible, the attempt to pursue the impossible as Derrida suggests, must resist any temptation to settle for a more acceptable and, perhaps easier outcome. Wright maintains that the task before us is to answer the challenge to take up the call to peace from the arriving university to come. It is a task that will forever remain before us despite all diligence, yet we have the opportunity to engage a future that may become the present through the act of stepping through and into the opening created within the university of the future. Wright suggests that peace, as opening, is the opening of peace. Wright argues that through a Derridean lens crafted from the Lévinasian other, a space is opened to and for peace within the imagined unconditional university. The deconstruction of the Other, in the non-space of différance, through différance, affords this opening, the opening of peace. Peace education, then, could embrace the difference of the Other and the third, overcoming its own inertia and onto-epistemological refusal within the provinciality of the university, and thereby, expand its capacity, scope, and legitimacy within the hallowed halls of academe. Peace education could discover its ontological voice in full multivocality through an investment in the development of many of the philosophical lenses presented herein. Wright maintains that we have the basic tools to accomplish this task as well as the knowledge to produce different, more specialized implements for our challenging work. Some of the lenses have already been fashioned and only need to be honed to reveal the image, while others await discovery. The responsibility of this work lies squarely on the shoulders of the professoriate as an open engagement with différance in the nexus of the cosmopolitical frame of our inter-subjectivity

In the final chapter, "The (Im)possibility of Trying for Reconciliation and Peace: The Significance of Conflict, Limits, and Exclusions in Transitional Democracy," Mario Di Paolantonio critiques the fact that various scholars of transitional democracy often justify the complex legacy of the "Trial of the Military" in Argentina by gesturing to its pedagogical ability to showcase the principles of deliberation and further reconciliation. In such a reading, the Trial is depicted as staging a public forum where post-conflict disagreements can be peacefully conciliated through an "educative dialogue" sustained by consensual regulative principles inherent in court procedures. The chapter takes issue with this reading by pointing to the limits and problems of understanding the pedagogical effects of the Trial through the discourses of peace and reconciliation. Di Paolantonio argues that an interpretative model that seeks to explain the Trial by emphasizing the conciliatory effects of an "educative dialogue" overlooks the significant role that conflict plays in the struggle to structure the legacy of this Trial. Moving beyond the attempt to dissolve conflict through dialogue and reconciliation allows him to elucidate the unsettled aspirations of the Trial as a pedagogical resource for contesting the immanence of a politics of containment. This critique speaks to recent events in Argentina where, despite previous attempts by the state to contain and overwrite the implications of the Trial (through various amnesty laws and pardons), the possibility of prosecuting past human rights violations has once again gained momentum in the courts. In order to appreciate the significance of the recent legal endeavors, the chapter underscores how the very contestation unleashed by the betrayed hopes of the Trial provides the public impetus for bringing the unsettled past wrongs before the law.

References

Anderson, G. (1985). "Competing Views of Human Nature in the Politics of Peace: Integrating Ideas of Cobb, Galtung, Gewirth, and Tillich,"*Dissertation Abstracts International*, 47(02), 560. (UMI No. 8607818).

Apple, M. (1990). *Ideology and Curriculum* (2nd ed.). New York and London: Routledge.

de Freitas, L., Morin, E. and Nicolescu, B. (Eds.). (1994). *Charter of Transdisciplinarity*, trans. K.-C. Voss. CIRET, International Center for Transdisciplinary Research. Available at: http://nicol.club.fr/ciret/english/charten.htm.

Derrida, J. (1990). *Du droit à la philosophie*. Paris: Galilée.

Dewey, J. (1916). *Democracy and Education: An introduction to the philosophy of education*. New York: The Macmillan Company.

Galtung, J. (2004). *Transcend and Transform: An introduction to conflict work*. Boulder, CO: Paradigm Publishers.

Gur-Ze'ev, I. (2001). "Philosophy of Peace Education in a Postmodern Era," *Educational Theory*, 51(3), 315–35.

Harris, I. (2004). "Peace Education Theory," Journal of Peace Education, 1(1), 5–20.

Harris, I. and Morrison, M. (2003). *Peace Education* (2nd ed.). Jefferson, NC: McFarland and Company, Inc.

Reardon, B. (1988). *Comprehensive Peace Education: Educating for global responsibility*. New York: Teachers College Press.

——(1999). Peace Education: A review and projection, Peace Education Reports 17. Malmö, Sweden: Lund University, Dept. of Educational and Psychological Research.

——(2001). *Education for a Culture of Peace in a Gender Perspective*. Paris: UNESCO Publishing, The Teacher's Library.

Salomon, G. (2006). "Does Peace Education Really Make a Difference?" Peace and Conflict: Journal of Peace Psychology, 12(1), 37–48.

Trifonas, P. (2000a). *The Ethics of Writing: Derrida, deconstruction and pedagogy*. Lanham, MD: Rowman and Littlefield Publishers.

——(Ed.). (2000b). *Revolutionary Pedagogies: Cultural politics, the institution of education, and the discourse of theory*. New York and London: Routledge Falmer.

——(2003). *Pedagogies of Difference: Rethinking education for social justice*. New York and London: Routledge Falmer.

1 Educational Reform and the Project of Militarization

Brian W. Lagotte and Michael W. Apple

The continuing struggle to expand the space and influence of critical peace education is crucial. But the efforts to build this movement do not occur on pristine soil. To be successful, they must deal with the ways in which the terrain of education is already being creatively filled by hegemonic policies and practices that seek to make militarization in education not only acceptable but seen as something that is a "positive reform," especially for economically dispossessed students. As one of us has argued elsewhere, at times, critical educational policies and practices are not sufficiently grounded in an understanding of the realities of the neoliberal and neoconservative reconstruction of education and of all things social. Nor do they fully understand the ways in which our common sense has been altered so that what counts as a "good" education, as a necessary reform, as legitimate knowledge, and as important evidence of success increasingly exists on the terrain constructed by dominant groups (Apple, 2000, 2006).

We wish to give a concrete example of what is happening in this regard, one in which the very opposite of peace—the militarization of school experiences—is sutured directly into educational reform in the United States. The example we shall detail is No Child Left Behind (NCLB) in the United States and the militaristic activities it has helped spawn and legitimate. As we shall show, this reform combines neoliberal visions of markets, privatization, and choice, with the strict regimes of accountability associated with new managerial approaches, and finally with neoconservative visions of the connections between military strength and the defense of "the Western Tradition" and empire. It has also led to the rise of sophisticated attempts at marketing the military in ways that make the development of critical educational policies and practices even more imperative.

NEOLIBERAL CURRICULUM AND PEDAGOGY

Let us begin our discussion with an outline of NCLB's neoliberal approach to educational reform. The neoliberal elements in NCLB are founded on the concept that the market is the best model for our public institutions and for society as a whole. For example, NCLB utilizes concepts such a standards, competition, and accountability to drive schools towards higher performance. Schooling, hence, is not only treated as a business; it becomes one.

In the broad view of this model, for example, for-profit charter schools begin to compete with public schools for student enrollment. This move is promoted as "providing parents more choice" for their children's education needs. These charter schools market themselves as being more efficient or higher quality than the public alternative to attract customers. Recently, more and more "brands" have entered the education market, like KIPP and the Education Innovation Laboratory. The recent reform of the later program is paying students to get good grades (Hernandez, 2008; Sadovi, 2008). On this level of analysis, the identity of the school shifts to being an "education service provider" and works to be competitive in the education market so individual schools will be the choice of education consumers (i.e. parents). According to this philosophy, competition is the key mechanism to eliminate "failing schools" and "unqualified teachers." And test scores are the only marker of what counts as success.

A more direct effect of this perspective on students is found in schools and classrooms. Teachers and students are now under enormous pressure through standardized testing to produce high, quantifiable results. Quantification is essential, because the new regime of managerialism requires that things be forever counted and measured. If it cannot be measured, then it cannot be evaluated, and therefore the effectiveness cannot be determined. The tests become the ultimate goal of education, and school funding is very much connected to how well students can achieve in these exams (Apple, 2006; Valenzuela, 2005). Education turns away from one of its most important goals, to inform a democratic society and create a critical citizenry.

But what is at stake here is not "simply" the role of schooling in the education of critically democratic citizens. This very process creates a different vision of youth and their role in our society. Youth are positioned as consumers and targets for aggressive marketing, as future workers, and as resources (or impediments) for the production of high test scores. But for many students, they are also increasingly seen as resources of another kind— as soldiers who will defend the aggressive expansion of the mythical free market by providing necessary muscle to open and protect trade agreements. Indeed, one of the lesser known aspects of NCLB is the opening it gives to aggressive military recruitment in schools.

Neoliberalism is not alone here. As one of us has argued elsewhere, NCLB incorporates key aspects of the neoconservative agenda as well (Apple, 2006). Its policy of standardizing a curriculum of facts in such a way that "the tail of the test wags the dog of the teacher" has created unresponsive and boring test prep curricula. This in essence amounts to what might be called a giant "push out" program in which large numbers of students are alienated from schools. Teachers who hope to introduce alternative voices in the classroom through more creative and critical curriculum find time is incredibly scarce due to test preparation. This is especially the case for working-class, poor, and minoritized youth (Gillborn, 2008; Valenzuela, 2005).

This emphasis on facts coheres with neoconservative educational proposals advanced by people such as E. D. Hirsch and others who argue for a restoration of reductive visions of "core knowledge" (Hirsch, 1987). And even though such proposals have been rigorously criticized (see Buras, 2008), this has not significantly interrupted their increasing influence in a time of very real worries among parents. The fact that all of this is occurring during one of the worst economic crises the world has experienced in many decades creates something of a perfect storm in which neoliberalism, neoconservatism, and new managerialism gain increasing salience in the minds of the public. It also creates an even wider opening for militarization and an acceptance of neoconservatism's defense of empire, as we shall soon see.

NEOCONSERVATISM AND THE MILITARIZATION OF EDUCATION

The neoconservative project extends past domestic venues to promote very aggressive foreign policies. The factions within the neoconservative movement that influence military recruiting policies form a political group promoting the Project for the New American Century. The motivation of the group is clear from their Statement of Purpose, found on their website at www.new-americancentury.org. The group laments the loss of Reagan-era principles supporting an expansion of the military and boldly projecting American principles abroad. They have four fundamental proposals for foreign policy: (1) significantly increase military spending; (2) strengthen ties with democratic allies and engage hostile regimes; (3) promote global economic and political freedom; and (4) accept "our responsibility" to preserve and extend a world order in line with America's principles and prosperity. This statement, and the majority of letters the group pens, are signed by such recognizable names as William Bennett, Jeb Bush, Dick Cheney, Donald Rumsfeld, Paul Wolfowitz, and others. These goals best represent the twenty-first-century style of imperialism that drove American foreign policy for a large portion of the twentieth century.

The neoconservative project of a greatly expanded, active military requires an extremely effective recruiting program. As the United States is involved in a violent war in Iraq and promises an escalated engagement in Afghanistan, attracting volunteers to the armed services is proving difficult. One consequence is an expanded public relations campaign to package a military career as a desirable service that will be actively chosen by student "consumers."

How does this affect education? In order to answer this, we need to return to NCLB. Beyond the aggressive corporatist project of high-stakes testing and punitive measures, which put an enormous strain on schools in low-income neighborhoods, NCLB promotes the direct military recruiting of students on school campuses and militarizes a good deal of school experience for identifiable groups of students. This militarism includes recruiters, but extends to include military representatives teaching in the classroom and a normalized presence of JROTC (Junior Reserve Officer Training Corps) programs (Giroux, 2004: 212). We agree with Furumoto (2005) when she defines school militarization as "practices and policies that orient youth towards military enlistment and service." She argues that these business and military friendly policies "serve to maintain the power and domination of the ruling capitalist class and diminish youth's agency and capacity to critique and engage authentically in society" (ibid.: 200).

The specifics of this are worth our attention. When the Elementary Education Act (NCLB) was renewed in 2001, Section 9528 was added to require any high school receiving federal funds to acquiesce to military "requirements" in two fundamental ways (Furumoto, 2005; Zgonjanin, 2006). First, for campus visits, high schools must provide military recruiters access equal to college or career recruiters. Second, high schools are required to submit all student directory information (name, address, and telephone number) to the Pentagon or have their federal funding revoked (McLaren and Jaramillo, 2004; Walsh, 2007). These policies are separate from the United States Department of Defense (DoD) provisions that compile directory information for recruiting (Feder, 2008).

The recruiting amendment contains regulations for opting out of the program that mandate the "local educational agency or private school [to] notify parents of their right to make such a request" (Feder, 2008: 132; Walsh, 2007). Unfortunately, school districts are interpreting these obligations in different ways, and the type of notice schools send to parents is proving to be the subject of much discussion. A "reasonable" method can possibly appear as a mailing notice (with a pile of other forms), as a paragraph buried in a student handbook, or as a portion of a school calendar (Holm, 2007; Walsh, 2007). Accountability to these vague regulations is further complicated by a lack of any monitoring system (Zgonjanin, 2006: 175). Therefore, there is an uneven process of educating parents on the military policies affecting their children.

This lack of oversight also includes the introduction of Section 9528. Much of the debate went on behind closed doors (McLaren and Jaramillo, 2004: 280) until Representatives David Vitter from Louisiana and Pete Sessions from Texas brought the amendment to the House floor (Zgonjanin, 2006). Vitter introduced the bill to prevent discrimination against the military by institutions that accepted federal funding. Providing no particular evidence, Vitter claimed that military recruiters "face daunting challenges in beefing up our military with good, new, young recruits" (ibid.: 171). "What is going on clearly, Mr. Chairman, is pure, old-fashioned bad political correctness and antimilitary ideology being shoved down the throats of our young people" (CR 147 – H2535). In an interview, Vitter stated that he "simply objected to high schools being able to deny a recruiter access to their students"

(Goodman, 2004: 5). Not once did the argument on the floor address the link between educational achievement and military recruiting. The speeches on the floor were clearly less about promoting rich democratic debate over a controversial policy and more about the promotion of particular conservative policy.

The lack of transparency in schools and in government surrounding this project demonstrates worrisome trends toward the rationing and manipulation of knowledge. This involves both military activity in high schools and a large data collection project initiated by the United States DoD. Each aspect of these programs is kept away from much scrutiny (ibid.). This information sharing and recruiters' access to high school campuses are mandates to be obeyed at the expense of losing federal monies (McLaren et al., 2004: 134). Few parents are aware of these aspects of NCLB, nor do they realize that they can complete a form that allows the student to "opt out" of the data collection. "Choice" requires information and it has become increasingly clear that the information on opting out is nearly invisible in many schools. Thus, in reality, for most parents there is no way for parents to avoid the proselytizing school visits by military recruiters.

RECRUITING SALES TACTICS

How does this system work? Dr. Gary Evans, through his outline of various recruiting practices targeting teenagers, highlights many areas of concern regarding the relationship among neoliberal tendencies, the military, and public schooling. He proposes that "the people in power today systematically use armed services recruiters—motivated by rank and bonus—as the agents of control and manipulation of US youth" (Evans, 2008). The people in power are specifically those actors most deeply involved in the foreign adventures that require a larger and growing military force. Generally it means those neoconservatives listed above and others associated with their project; including, of course, the Secretary of Defense and the Secretary of Education.

At the time the recruiting practices that Evans critiques gained speed, these two offices were filled by former Secretary of Defense Donald Rumsfeld and former Secretary of Education Rod Paige. In a letter to colleagues in the defense and education fields, they write that America supports a heritage of "defending freedom" with an all-volunteer military force. To protect that heritage, "requires the active support of public institutions in presenting military opportunities to our young people for their consideration" (Paige and Rumsfeld, 2002). After reviewing the outline of the 2001 NCLB and 2002 National Defense Authorization provisions on collecting high-school student information, Paige and Rumsfeld ask for educators' assistance because the military may be the best opportunity for "some of our students" to get a college education. They close by emphasizing their military careers and their work in the executive office to illustrate the opportunities the armed services offer.

The systematic use of military recruiters that Evans mentions is clearly fashioned around the neoliberal impulse to turn everything into a commodity to be marketed, bought, and sold. It is a sales campaign in which the recruiters are intensely pressured to make quota for new applicants. The first step of any successful sales campaign is for military representatives to discover which students could be most receptive to a sales presentation. In pursuit of this goal, the military uses a system to "pre-qualify" individuals for military service by determining who will meet the requirements for application. Adding to the regimented program of NCLB, the military has their own standardized test for these goals.

Since Vietnam, the Army has taken advantage of a number of multiple-choice, standardized tests to sort, classify, and identify recruits. As listed on their website (http://www.military.com/ASVAB), the Armed Service Vocational Aptitude Battery test is a standardized exam that measures arithmetic reasoning, math knowledge, word knowledge, paragraph comprehension, and vocational elements. Reportedly, the scores on the exam can be useful not only to the military, but for vocational or university decisions. When one reads a bit further, however, the ASVAB is also referred to as the AFQT—the Armed Forces Qualification Test. The scores on the AFQT (i.e., the ASVAB) qualify an applicant for a military occupation in a variety of branches and can determine what type of position is best.

Although the test is available at recruiting offices, it is also often administered in the junior year of high school, with varying levels of transparency of intent, and varying interpretations of the fact it is an optional test. Ever sensitive to audience, the military carefully refers to the exam in schools with a more subtle name of "aptitude" rather than explicitly acknowledging that it is for "qualification." The test, which is described as merely a measure of a student's potential for a variety of careers, is a powerful tool for military recruiters. Although the test is administered, as one DoD official has claimed, as a "public service," it is also "well known as an aptitude screen for military recruitment" (Hardy and Purcell, 2008). But, like other information-gathering projects through NCLB, parents are again often uninformed on how to opt their children out of the test, nor do they always know when the test is being administered. It is unlikely that they recognize (and a candid DoD document admits) that the exam is to "provide the military services with access to the high school market and recruiters with prequalified recruiting leads" (ibid.). Notice the shift to neoliberal phrasings: "high school market," "prequalified," and "leads."

The ASVAB/AFQT exam, therefore, serves both needs of military recruiters. It begins the enormous data-collection process by gaining student contact information and their individual strengths and weaknesses. It is an initial survey to assist recruiters in shaping their sales message accordingly. Second, it "pre-qualifies applicants" since the branches of the armed services require a certain score on the test. The exam helps recruiters eliminate those useless contacts and streamline their market base for targeting. We want to be clear that the terminology we are using to explain the strategies and tactics of military recruiting is not an assumption. We are not speaking of the "school market" and recruiting "sales calls" as a metaphor. This is how officials in the DoD explicitly understand their project. Markets and sales pitches are the terms that recruiting command itself uses when training field officers in their duties.

This language can be lifted directly from the School Recruiting Program (SRP) Handbook. This handbook is produced by United States Army Recruiting Command to give recruiters a single document of best practices for use in schools:

> It is designed to assist recruiters in penetrating their school market and channeling their efforts through specific tasks and goals to obtain the maximum number of quality enlistments. The SRP is also an important part of an integrated recruiting prospecting-lead generation program that ensures total market penetration.
>
> (Morris, 2004)

The school system, then, is envisioned as another market to access. More specifically, schools themselves are meticulously screened to find the best possible opportunity for recruiters, i.e., low-income urban or rural schools (Herbert, 2005). The schools are then targeted with a marketing plan that fits their assigned identity.

Parts of the handbook reads as a sales manual for a product that may, at times, receive a harsh reception on a cold call. The first step, of course, is to get one's foot in the door and to "own the school" by developing a good rapport from the onset is essential. "This is a basic step in the sales process and a prerequisite to an effective school program" (Morris, 2004). After recruiters have laid the appropriate foundation and have gained control of the particular school market, they must be diligent or they may "relinquish ownership to the other services if we fail to maintain a strong SRP" (ibid.). Though not defined, the language implies that the different branches of the military battle to gain control of various high schools to each meet their individual quotas. As competition is an essential element of a market-based system, this should not surprise us.

After recruiters gain access to a high school and the students, faculty, and administrators become comfortable with their presence, they must turn to the task at hand. The first step is to match the product to customer need. For a military recruiter in a high school, this means determining how the school designs its curriculum and long-term goals. "An effective sales approach would be to tailor a program to fit the needs and interests of the individual school" (ibid.). The recruiter should then begin contacting students in the summer before their senior year, again after school begins, and finally for a third time in early spring. But, recruiters need not follow this strict timeline, and if needed, recruiters "can make an appointment for a sales presentation on the first contact" because the timing of the presentation is important since recruiters "will probably need to tailor [their] sales message to meet the stage" of the school year (ibid.). The military representative, therefore, is not providing objective information to help students decide between the armed services, entering the civilian workplace, or attending college. The recruiters are in essence high-powered sales personnel, functioning as if they have to move used cars off the lot (McCarthy, 2005). The school is a market.

DIRECT MARKETING A MILITARY CAREER

Even though NCLB provided a major widening of the space where military recruiting can go on and linked it directly to the process of building "more responsive" educational reforms, the marketing efforts go well beyond NCLB. For total market saturation, corporations rely on sophisticated advertising strategies linked to large customer databases. The armed forces are no different. The Pentagon maintains several databases with information that is often integrated to more accurately target specific markets. The most popular of these is the Joint Advertising and Market Research & Studies (JAMRS) database, which is a clearing house for a variety of student information. What type of information is available, and who maintains the database, are far from transparent. Originally, the data collected were from multiple sources such as selective service, the Department of Motor Vehicles, and purchasing collections from private data services. Furthermore, the database consisted of highly private information such as ethnicity, social security numbers, and grade point average until a New York Civil Liberties Union lawsuit forced the Pentagon to limit their data to directory information (NYCLU, 2007).

At the onset, the PR house Leo Barnett controlled the data and marketing strategy of the United States Army and the JAMRS database. A key aspect of the Barnett strategy was direct advertising, a marketing approach with a more targeted focus. According to an executive pitching to the Army, this "customer relationship management" was going to be the "future of all recruiting advertising" (Arndorfer, 2005a). Narrowing the market is key to this, since in order for the military to determine how to target, it must know the characteristics of those teens who are most likely to sign up for the military (Arndorfer, 2005b). After determining the audience, the marketer needs to find the access points to these youth. The Pentagon uses their software system to collect and disaggregate the data on all new recruits and applicants. Officials then dice this information into 66 different categories in order to "reach target markets and assist in the development of more effective marketing messages and incentive policies" (Arndorfer, 2005a). Then, with this information, Leo Barnett's sophisticated marketing programs begin to construct new identities of the youth they are targeting.

The disaggregated data of a marketing database perpetuates powerful stereotypes. For example, there is the "down-in-the-city" type, which consists of urban, black and Latino, low-income households with a high school degree as the highest educational attainment. This "type" reads Jet and Vibe magazines and eats at White Castle and Checkers (ibid.). With this group defined, the work now turns to a marketing message ("for those who have no other option") and various advertising campaigns located in the access points (Jet magazine) identified by the software tools. These messages are tailored and polished by all the sophisticated marketing methods of contemporary corporate public relations. And, of course, this information is by no means a comprehensive presentation of all the complex consequences of choosing the Army as a career opportunity.

Recently, the DoD switched to, and then renewed a one-year contract with, Mullen Public Relations. This 50 million contract appointed Mullen as the Agency of Record (AOR) for the JAMRS program, authorizing it to buy media spots in various locations on behalf of the Pentagon (McKenna, 2007). This PR firm is responsible for campaigns such as the www.todaysmilitary. com website, the magazine Futures, and a recent "documentary" produced on careers in the armed forces entitled Today's Military: Extraordinary People, Extraordinary Opportunities. Mullen is a unit within the larger global Interpublic Group marketing conglomerate and is a well-known AOR for leading corporate brands. Thus, the Army account serves as merely one other "product line" that requires a honed message and image to market. The "Today's Military" campaign, for example, is targeting adults who may influence teens to join military service.

Another example of a commercial produced by Mullen shows how well advertising sutures together marketing, the military, and corporate America seamlessly by featuring Donald Trump and Kelly Perdew. Perdew was the second-season winner of Trump's reality business show and is also a retired Army Ranger. Perdew often spoke of his military career in relation to his business success throughout the season, and the commercial taps into this image (Adweek, 2005). The 30-second spot shows both Trump and Perdew in a skyscraper boardroom, but overlays images of soldiers descending from Blackhawk helicopters and cruising in Zodiac patrol boats. The message, especially in the current time of economic stress, is that military training is an essential component to prepare for a successful business career. Mullen PR and the Pentagon are continually searching for easy access to a large audience of teens who can view these commercial spots.

An alternative strategy to the narrowly targeted distribution is to collect as many viewers as possible and fill as much of the available time with your material. A perfect, ready-made tool for targeting a large teen audience is Channel One. Channel One is a news network that generates materials specifically for teens, and is broadcast in 12-minute segments in schools across the United States (see Apple, 2000). According to the "About Us" page of their website (www.channelone.com), their coverage includes "more than 6 million teens in middle schools and high schools across the country." They gain access to these school by providing free television and satellite reception technology.

In exchange, schools must broadcast the Channel One show every day to a large majority of students in their school. The purpose, Channel One claims, is "is to spark debate and discussion among teens, and also discussion between young people and their parents and educators, on the important issues affecting young people in America." Debate and discussion are sparked by the 10 minutes of news stories on each broadcast. The other two minutes, however, consist entirely of advertisements (Hays, 1999). These are usually broadcast in two different commercial breaks.

For this reason, Channel One has been under close scrutiny and critique by a number of scholars and policy experts (see e.g. Apple, 2000). While this material is too vast to be reviewed in this chapter, the arguments center around privacy and the role of commercialism within the school walls. Critics argue, correctly we believe, that our children need not be sold to global corporations in exchange for television equipment. There is something deeply troubling about children being treated as a captive audience "for sale" in the first place. But this new identity of the individual as consumer in the neoliberal mindset has clearly found its way into schools and has begun to supplant the identity of child as student. We do not wish to simply repeat the arguments that Channel One represents a commercialization of the school space, although of course it does. Rather, our argument is that the military has adopted this market-based mentality to sell itself to students and is currently colonizing these already constructed commercial spaces.

The United States Army has been taking full advantage of the resources and audience that Channel One has to offer. As early as 2005, when the growth of the network began to slow, the Army's advertising helped buoy the company. In the first quarter of 2005, it was the Army, along with cell phone and video game companies, that help boost Channel One's revenues by 2 percent (Borja, 2005). This revenue may result from the fact that the Army saturates as much of the broadcast as possible. An informal journal kept by a high school student shows that each day at least one military advertisement appears in the commercial break, and sometimes two appear back to back (Whitehurst, 2005). The Army also sponsors the daily "pop quiz" trivia challenge; it is mentioned in the introduction, and its emblem appears on the screen for the duration of the quiz. The Army and Channel One are co-sponsors for an entire section of video spotlights called "Finding Strength." Within this spotlight, some videos were produced to highlight the military itself, for example, "Cell Phones for Soldiers." Furthermore, early in the "Army of One" sales campaign, the Army even produced webisodes on the lives of fresh recruits (Business Wire, 2001). These spots were broadcast weekly through Channel One and other media outlets.

Reviewing the above information, one can imagine what a possible Channel One broadcast could look like in an average middle school in the United States. Within a 12-minute span of time, the captive audience of 7th, 8th, and perhaps 9th graders can be subject to multiple messages of the military advertising campaign. During the news broadcast they can view spotlight videos of various military adventures sponsored by the United States Army. The news section ends with a trivia quiz, again sponsored by the United States Army. The program then breaks for commercials, which, of course, are bought by the United States armed forces. This is most likely what the School Recruiting Program Handbook above meant by "total market penetration." In this way, the school itself becomes a key center for the distribution of particular messages to particular youth. NCLB's hidden elements open up the space to make this even more legitimate. It is this set of hidden elements and the messages embodied in them that are participating in the construction of a new common sense about what schools are for and who controls what we teach our youth. This is the challenge that critical peace education must cope with if it is to seriously contest these emerging ideological forms.

CONCLUSION

In this chapter, we have situated the little known but steadily increasing militarization of schooling back into the ways in which specific kinds of educational reform operate. By focusing on the ways in which NCLB made military recruitment even more legitimate, indeed nearly mandatory, at the same time as it created even more dismal educational experiences for economically dispossessed youth in a time when jobs are rapidly disappearing, we have shown how it has both helped to spawn and bring together the generation of a system of public relations, marketing, and database manipulation. This has been complemented by a neoliberal market-based mentality that has been adopted wholesale by the military to recruit youth through high schools in the United States. The language articulated by the leaders in the recruiting command of sales calls and market saturation, linked to the complex and slick marketing projects designed and implemented by some of the largest global firms, illustrates the danger of this type of relationship.

What does this mean for a vision of a truly rich and critically democratic model of education? What does it mean when education is reduced to advertising? As Alex Molnar's (2005) work on school commercialism demonstrates, when education becomes increasingly a site of mass marketing, this largely benefits economically powerful groups, often at the expense of the larger group of less powerful citizens. For critical educators, it also clearly represents a very conservative pedagogical model, a mode of instruction that imposes information from the top down. Advertisements-as-education are provided for consumption; there is no joint construction of the knowledge.

In this form of pedagogy, new definitions of "legitimate" knowledge and "legitimate" futures are put in place not to educate, but to manipulate. The messages that are broadcast are researched, tested in focus groups, and previewed in specific markets before being presented to the public. The media-as-educator creates conditions that seek to have individuals take on new identities—especially students with few career opportunities—and to behave in particular ways. "I am an Army of One, defending America." What this means in terms of the neoconservative agenda of empire is invisible, as is the less than stellar presence of the United States in the defense of "our" markets and "our" place in the world. An education in which so many individuals cannot critically reflect on their own choices and on the role of empire and the military's role in its maintenance is not part of this agenda. Unless the movement to develop and institute models of critical peace education thinks tactically about what is already happening, and unless they connect to movements to challenge the economic conditions that make the military seem to so many dispossessed youth as the only choice they realistically have, they will have little success. This will not be simple. But whoever said that struggling against dominance would be easy?

References

Adweek (2005). "Mullen's got 'What it Takes' for JAMRS."

Apple, M. W. (2000). *Official Knowledge: Democratic education in a conservative age* (2nd ed.). New York: Routledge.

——(2006). *Educating the "Right" Way: Markets, standards, God, and inequality* (2nd ed.). New York: Routledge.

Arndorfer, J. B. (2005a). "Army Looking for a Direct Hit.,"Advertising Age, July 11, p. 4.

——(2005b). "Target Practice," Advertising Age, November 28, p. 1.

Borja, R. (2005). "Channel One Struggling in Shifting Market," Education Week, 24 (43), 3, 14.

Buras, K. L. (2008). *Rightist Multiculturalism: Core lessons on neoconservative school reform*. New York: Routledge.

Business Wire (2001). "Army Launches Second Phase of 'Army of One.'" February 3.

Evans, G. (2008). "Recruiting Children into the US Military." Available at: http://www.ringnebula.com/Oil/recruiting-children.htm (accessed September 23).

Feder, J. (2008). "Military Recruitment Provisions Under the No Child Left Behind Act: A Legal Analysis," in P. H. Berkhart (Ed.), *No Child Left Behind: Issues and developments*. New York: Nova Science Publishers.

Furumoto, R. (2005). "No Poor Child Left Unrecruited: How N.C.L.B. Codifies and Perpetuates Urban School Militarism," Equity & Excellence in Education, 38, 200–10.

Gillborn, D. (2008). *Racism and Education: Accident or conspiracy*. London: Routledge.

Giroux, H. A. (2004). "War on Terror: The Militarising of Public Space and Culture in the United States," Third Text, 18(4), 211–21.

Goodman, D. (2004). "N.C.L.B. Accesses High-Schoolers for the Military in War Time," Education Digest, 69(9), 4–6.

Hardy, D. and Purcell, D. (2008). "Growing Hesitancy over a Military Test,". The Philadelphia Inquirer, August 6, p. B01.

Hays, C. (1999). "Channel One's Mixed Grades in Schools," The New York Times, December 5.

Herbert, B. (2005). "Uncle Sam Really Wants You," The New York Times, June 16, p. 27.

Hernandez, J. (2008). "New Effort Aims to Test Theories of Education," The New York Times, September 25, p. B6.

Hirsch, E. D. (1987). *Cultural Literacy: What every American needs to know.* Boston: Houghton Mifflin.

Holm, K. D. (2007). "No Child Left Behind and Military Recruitment in High Schools: When Privacy Rights Trump a Legitimate Government Interest," Journal of Law & Education, 36(4), 581–88.

McCarthy, S. (2005). " 'Making Mission' in a Tough Market," The Globe and Mail, December 10, p. 23.

McKenna, T. (2007). "DoD Renews Contract with Mullen PR," PR Week, June 18.

McLaren, P. and Jaramillo, N. (2004). "Neoliberal Citizenship, the New Imperialism, and Federal Education Policy," in J. O'Donnell, M. Pruyn, and R. C. Chavez (Eds.), *Social Justice in These Times.* Greenwich, CT: Information Age Publishing.

McLaren, P., Martin, G., Farahmandpur, R., and Jaramillo, N. (2004). "Teaching in and against Empire: Critical Pedagogy as Revolutionary Praxis," Teacher Education Quarterly, 31(1), 131–53.

Molnar, A. (2005). *School Commercialism: From democratic ideal to market commodity.* New York: Routledge.

Morris, B. D. (2004). *School Recruiting Program Handbook.* Available at: http://www. usarec.army.mil/im/formpub/Pubs.htm#pamphlets.

NYCLU (2007). "To Settle N.Y.C.L.U. Lawsuit, Defense Department Reforms Student Military Recruiting Database." Available at: http://www.nyclu.org/node/130 (accessed December 27, 2008).

Paige, R., and Rumsfeld, D. (2002). "Recruiting Letter." Available at: http://www.ed. gov/news/pressreleases/2002/10/recruitingletter.html.

Sadovi, C. (2008). "More than 1,650 CPS Students Paid for Good Grades," Chicago Tribune, October 17.

Valenzuela, A. (2005). *Leaving Children Behind: How "Texas-style" accountability fails Latino youth.* Albany: State University of New York Press.

Walsh, M. (2007). *What Do I Do When – : The answer book on the No Child Left Behind Act.* Horsham, PA: LRP Publications.

Whitehurst, T. (2005). "Military Recruiting on Channel One." Available at: http:// www.counterpunch.org/whitehurst02212005.html (accessed December 12, 2008).

Zgonjanin, S. (2006). "No Child Left (Behind) Unrecruited," Connecticut Public Interest Law Journal, 5(2), 167–95.

2 Encountering Peace

The Politics of Participation when Educating for Co-Existence

Maria Hantzopoulos

In recent years, co-existence dialogue programs among groups whose people or nations have been engaged in conflict have proliferated in all corners of the globe. Often these enterprises come in the form of summer camps or joint endeavors, aimed at bringing together youth and children, though many also convene adults. Many of these programs function outside of the actual physical context of conflict on more ostensibly "neutral" grounds, while others convene people in what some consider the heart of the conflicted terrain. While such co-existence initiatives often vary in scope and mission, most share a common aim and purpose: to facilitate dialogue among members of the identified conflicting groups in the hopes of eventually attaining peaceful reconciliation (operating under the assumption that this is a desired and agreed upon goal).

The core and fundamental notion of dialogue in these peace education programs is a seemingly innocuous and often taken-for-granted method; one that is an unsaid means for building and equalizing relationships, humanizing the 'Other,' and moving towards an ideal state of 'peace' and 'understanding' among groups that are engaged in 'conflict.' While many scholars acknowledge some limitations of these initiatives, most research on such programs remains optimistic and still highlights the beneficial nature of fostering dialogue and their potential ability to build peace (see Abu-Nimmer, 2004; Bar-Tal, 2004; Dahl, 2009; Feuerverger, 2001; Schimmel, 2009).

As these programs garner popularity, media attention, and funding, however, little attention is paid to who actually desires the need for dialogue. In fact, many would-be participants, ordinary members of civil society who are not necessarily aligned with hard-lined nationalist party politics, view these programs with skepticism. In part, this has to do with the fact that despite the ubiquity of such programs, actual peace often remains elusive, casting doubt on the efficacy and intentions of these endeavors. A recent Economist article went to the heart of this paradox, posing two provocative questions about co-existence initiatives among Israelis and Palestinians, "If so many people are intent on making peace, why hasn't it happened by now? Or more fairly: do such co-existence projects actually change anything for the good?" (2007). While these questions may viscerally cause some practitioners of peace educators to balk, they also reveal a phenomenon that needs to be explored and probed further, particularly as various forms of violence continues to escalate worldwide (Amnesty International, 2009).

This chapter endeavors to think deeply about such questions by beginning to unpack this notion of dialogue as a process of and to peace, and interrogating the dominant discourses and assumptions often associated with the word peace. The reflections and insights about my own experiences as a co-existence dialogue facilitator are the initial catalyst for this inquiry, though conversations and interviews that shed light on potential participant resistance to dialogue groups, particularly when larger asymmetrical power relations define the broader landscape, have propelled this further analysis. Drawing from practical experience, post-structural and feminist theories, and participant interviews, this chapter carefully considers and offers a re-reading of key concepts such as dialogue and peace in these types of programs, raising questions about the assumptions embedded within these concepts. In particular, I investigate how they are defined, embodied, manifested, performed, and experienced, by whom and for what reason(s) and explore the normative and "commonsense" qualities that are inherent in these concepts to shed light on possible ways they operate to monitor, subjugate, and control ways of being and thinking.

EDUCATIONAL APPROACHES TO DIALOGUE AND PEACE: A BRIEF REVIEW

In the academic realm, peace education has only recently moved from a marginalized discipline into a more accepted and legitimized field, evidenced by the multitude of peace education programs, as well peace and conflict studies, worldwide. Despite this exponential increase, peace education is often described as a field that is elusive and lacking concrete definition (Bar-Tal, 2002; Danesh, 2006; Reardon, 2000). Many suggest the indefinable contours of the field emanate from the loose way in which it has emerged, evolving in a variety of specific socio- and political contexts, contingent upon the particular societal issues, conditions, resources and educator perspectives that exist (Bar-Tal, 2000; Harris, 2004; Reardon, 2000). Moreover, the concept of peace itself holds numerous cultural meanings in different cultures (Groff, 2002; Harris, 2004), contributing to the difficulty in creating concretized boundaries to the field and definitions of the discipline.

This boundless and almost haphazard nature of the field, however, has also contributed to its development. Most scholars and practitioners agree that peace education is really a multi-, inter- and trans-disciplinary field that encompasses many subfields, including human rights education, development education, conflict resolution education, disarmament education and environmental education (see Reardon, 2000; Bajaj, 2008; Harris, 2004). Recognizing the multitude of programs, research, and contexts in which peace education is studied, applied and researched, scholars have also come up with fluid definitions to help ground the field. Bajaj (2008) draws from Reardon (1988), Galtung (1969) and Toh (2006) to suggest that peace education is

> Generally defined as education policy, planning, pedagogy, and practice that can provide learners – in any setting – with the skills and values to work towards comprehensive peace. Comprehensive peace includes the oft discussed domains of both "negative" and positive peace that respectively comprise the abolition of direct or physical violence, and structural violence constituted by systematic inequalities that deprive individuals of the basic human rights.
>
> (Bajaj, 2008: 1–2)

In societies that have been engaged in what many describe as an "intractable" conflict, or in multicultural societies in which tensions among majority and minority groups run high, encounter groups are often the form of peace education employed. According to Salomon (2002), the purposes of contact or encounter programs depend on who is involved in them. For those from conflict-ridden contexts, the purpose is to develop a sense of mutual responsibility toward the 'Other' (and each other) by altering group members' pre-conceived perceptions of each other; for those in multicultural societies, the purpose is to foster understanding and collaboration, enhance equality and increase co-existence among group members (Salomon, 2002; Yablon, 2007). These programs are undergirded by the principle that face-to-face contact can ultimately "reduce inter-group tension and promote understanding between the groups" (Yablon, 2007: 4).

Dialogue is one of the central methods used in these encounter programs, though often project-oriented activities, such as art-making, sports, and joint tasks are also the premise to promote co-existence. In Freirean terms (see Freire 1972/1994), dialogical encounters form the basis of transforming student–teacher relationship into more egalitarian ones, with the hope that oppressive societal structures and relations will follow with a parallel equalizing transformation. Similarly, in encounter groups, dialogue also serves as a means towards transforming relationships among conflicting or minority/majority groups by creating spaces in which all parties are ostensibly granted equality of voice. These personal transformative relations would then translate into the broader societal context so that peaceful co-existence ensues in both spheres.

This chapter troubles these notions of dialogue and co-existence and specifically looks at how these means and goals, however loosely framed and contextually bound, are often fraught with tension, particularly when competing interests and larger structural inequities complicate localized (and often generalized) understandings of peace in the pursuit and attainment of co-existence. While scholars have acknowledged the diverse contexts in which peace education programs exist and flourish globally, there is also a general assumption that micro-level interactions among people in a conflicted area can transform macro-level asymmetries within that broader yet localized context (and conflict). Whether or not there may be some truth to this, this assumption does not question how these micro-level interactions might also be, in fact, beholden to the macro-level asymmetries. And while peace education assumes "an agreed upon universal respect for human dignity and rights" (Reardon, 2000), what are the hidden costs of bringing folks together from conflicting sides? How might dialogue obscure or ignore latent power dynamics among participants in the attainment of 'peace' and co-existence?

RE-THINKING THE PROMISE OF DIALOGUE: A PERSONAL REFLECTION

As mentioned earlier, my own experiences as a co-existence dialogue facilitator instigated this re-reading and challenged my own beliefs about peace, dialogue, and conflict resolution, elucidating some fundamental questions that were raised for me at that time. When I accepted a position to work with youth mostly from North and South Cyprus at a summer camp in the United States, I was incredibly excited about the possibilities that this might engender in terms of conflict transformation. Despite the fact that I had, at that point, never even been to Cyprus, I was hired not only because of my varied youth work experience in the U.S. in 'multicultural' contexts, but also because the North Cypriot co-facilitator who was also hired needed to be partnered with someone from the 'other side.' The fact that I have Greek ancestry and spoke Greek qualified me as such, though my connection to Cyprus was admittedly rather tenuous. While there were a couple of Greek, Turkish, and even one U.S. student who were part of the dialogue group (the first two as representatives of nationalities related to the conflict, and the latter as a neutral party—despite the historical role of the United States in the region), the sessions were dedicated to dialoguing about Cyprus and envisioning a different future than what was the status quo.

My co-facilitator and I had similar, though not identical, post-colonial readings of the 'conflict.' We agreed that the identities of 'Greek,' 'Turkish,' and 'Cypriot' (whether North or South), were partly constructed through European imperialism and colonialism of the nineteenth and twentieth centuries, and maintained in current nationalist agendas to preserve and privilege the somewhat arbitrary nation-states that were created after the collapse of the Ottoman Empire. In fact, after meeting each other and talking for some time, we were elated to start working together. I think naively, and perhaps disingenuously, we approached our work with the hope that the unveiling and revelations of historical and political truths would catapult these young people to challenge the status quo positions of their governments, reject the grand national narratives explicitly written in their textbooks, and transform them into advocates for peace and justice (which, in reality and retrospect, was our unspoken definition of peace and justice). In many ways, we ideologically agreed that the exposure of "truths" would naturally lead to such an outcome, even though it was never explicitly said.

It became apparent prior to the first session, however, that there were many problems with this tacit assumption, including both the pedagogical approaches, in which we diverged, and the teleological outcomes that he/I/we desired, which in fact, had been the real source of the dilemma. This manifested in both the disjuncture of our facilitation styles as well as in the (thankfully) unpredictable responses of the participants, who disrupted our trajectory towards mutual and common understanding.

As the sessions progressed, I began to realize that often the youth did not always respond in ways that I/we imagined and hoped they might and that they did not always come to the "peaceful" conclusion I/we had wished. Though we expected emotional and frustrated reactions to dialogue, we were not always prepared for the participant who simply would not engage.

This implied teleological transformation that I/we had desired, therefore, did not always manifest, regardless of whether driven by facilitator directives explicitly or by participant realities (and facilitator wishes implicitly). This was certainly not possible (nor, I now believe, even desirable) given the multiplicity of truths and experiences that converged in the room. Yet, what was more remarkable retrospectively was not so much the divergence away from 'peaceful resolution,' but rather, when the 'transformation' of a camper, to the satisfaction of my partner and me, displayed itself in a self-congratulatory manner before our eyes. While the sense of accomplishment we possessed over a participant's 'growth' felt very real in the moment, I often wondered in hindsight how much of it was real or how much of this was performed?[1] As the discourses surrounding what a peaceful (i.e. transformed, i.e. successful) camper circulated tacitly throughout the grounds, I could not help but wonder how much those discourses played into the way that students embraced and performed a particular identity.

Ultimately, these questions raise concerns about the discourses surrounding the notion of 'peace' itself that go beyond this particular experience to inform group and inter-personal dynamics in any contrived co-existence setting. Questions that complicate how peace is defined, embodied, manifested, performed, and experienced, by whom and for what reason(s), in what locales and at what time, are often completely ignored (perhaps even deliberately) in the well-intentioned design of such dialogue programs. While sometimes there is an attempt to acknowledge such types of questions, it is often superficial, and a thorough and rigorous interrogation of them is often sidelined in the name of unity toward a more peaceful future. Yet, evading such questions ignores how 'peace,' an imagined state that seemingly everyone covets and wants, brings forth its own normative and 'commonsense' qualities that potentially operate in ways to monitor, subjugate, and control behaviors and ways of being and thinking.

DIFFICULT DIALOGUES: THE CIRCULATION OF POWER IN CRITICAL CONVERSATIONS

Many scholars in the field of education have used Foucauldian notions of power not only to examine how conventional and accepted educational initiatives create subjects that are both disciplined and monitored (see Basu, 1997; Kohl, 2009), but also how seemingly progressive alternatives (that are endorsed categorically as better by their supporters) are in fact anything but emancipatory or transcendent (Ellsworth, 1989; Gore, 1992; Luke, 1992; Popkewitz, 1998; Bartlett, 2009).[2] Critical pedagogy, for instance, a type of educational vision that is grounded in the theoretical tradition of Neo-Marxist critical theory, has undergone a post-structural re-reading since the early 1990s.[3] Rooted in the concept of liberation, the overall goal of critical pedagogy has been to form a cohesive and democratizing educational agenda that enables subjugated masses to free themselves from the economic, political, and cultural structures that oppressed them (Luke, 1992). It is enacted through a dialogical process in which teachers engage students in recognizing their own experiences and identities, and use these as a catalyst for personal and societal transformation. Encounter programs and peace education, like critical pedagogy, also utilize dialogue as one of the tools for transformation (Reardon, 2000). In this case, inter-group dialogue is a way to move towards a world that embodies both negative and positive peace (Reardon, 2000, 2001; Harris and Morrison, 2003).[4]

Many of the critiques of critical pedagogy have focused on Freirean conceptions of dialogue, particularly the idealistic relationship that Freire posed between student and teacher (Bartlett, 2005; Schugurensky, 1998). The most scathing critiques, however, distrusted the feasibility of modern critical pedagogy's promise of transformation and complicated its core assumptions that privileged reason as the ultimate sphere upon which knowledge is constructed and transformation could take place. Post-structural scholars showed that these assumptions were inherently problematic, as they were embedded in liberal conceptions (equality, emancipation, and democracy) located within masculine notions of citizenship and rationality (see Gore, 1992; Luke, 1992). In particular, Ellsworth (1989), who partly based her critique, much like this one, on experiential evidence from a course she taught on anti-racist pedagogies, challenged the possibilities of dialogue. Through her reflections and interpretations of the course, which attempted to employ aspects of critical pedagogy such as "critical reflection," "student voice," "empowerment," and "dialogue," Ellsworth concluded that "key assumptions, goals, and pedagogical practices fundamental to literature on critical pedagogy ... are repressive myths that perpetuate relations of domination" (ibid.: 91).

While she found the literature on critical pedagogy de-contextualized and abstract, and thus, useless in its applicability, she was notably frustrated by how the employment of key concepts were contingent upon rational dialogical engagement, which, according to Ellsworth, has operated in ways that set up as opposite the irrational Other, which has been understood historically as the province of women and other exotic Others. In schools, rational deliberation, reflection, and consideration of all viewpoints have become a vehicle for regulating conflict and the power to speak.

(ibid.: 308)

This emphasis on rational dialogue, moreover, denied that thought was bound to discourse instead of reason, thereby disallowing the construction of partial narratives that were less totalizing and singular.

As a result of such critiques, some scholars have also pointed the impossibility of egalitarian dialogue and have advocated abandoning the critical pedagogy project all together. For instance, in discussing "democratic dialogue," Boler (2000) argues that there can actually be no such thing when power inequities that exist in society-at-large are reflected through the microcosm of the classroom. Rather than struggling to achieve egalitarian participation in the classroom, she abandons attempts for dialogical action and critical pedagogy by urging for an affirmative action pedagogy that seeks to redress inequality in a different way. Since voices are marginalized through institutional racism, sexism, classism, and corporate control, she asserts that this type of pedagogy "recognizes that we are not equally protected in practice by the First Amendment, and that education needs to fairly represent marginalized voices by challenging dominant voices in the classroom" (ibid.: 322). As a result, Boler believes that historically marginalized voices should be privileged in the classroom, even if this means restricting the voices of the historically (and presently) dominant. She provides varied examples of this type of pedagogy, ranging from prohibiting men from a women's studies classroom, to creating open discussions in which comments are challenged through critical analysis, to setting up "ground rules" for course enrollment.

Others, like Jones (2004), raise issue with the ways that dialogue functions in the classroom to keep power located in the hands of the 'dominant' actors. Drawing from her experiences and research with her white and non-white students, she suggests that the desire for dialogue tacitly maintains and reproduces colonial relationships. She states that although the calls for dialogue suggest that it is about "hearing each other," the positionality of each group really suggests that it is about "the dominant hearing the marginalized other." She argues that since members of marginalized groups are immersed in and hear the dominant world view daily, there is no need for them to hear the other perspective. Thus, the dominant are the central actors (of hearing) and dialogue provides access for them to the lives and experiences of the marginalized Other. Jones contends that in democratic dialogue, the marginalized ultimately "speak for our benefit in that they meet our desires to understand, and their speech is granted by our hearing" (ibid.: 66). In this sense, the dialogical relationship remains unegalitarian.

THE (UN)INTENDED CONSEQUENCES OF 'DOING' DIALOGUE: A COULD-BE PARTICIPANT PERSPECTIVE

What are the implications of these types of critiques for peace education and co-existence type programs? Since dialogue is a central method in these endeavors, similar questions that trouble the ways in which power circulates among participants need to be raised. Moreover, the concept and rhetoric of peace in these programs evoke a similar teleological connotation that is present with discourses surrounding emancipation and liberation in critical pedagogy. As one can ask the critical pedagogue, for whom really is this notion of freedom and by whom is it really defined? One can also ask the peace educator and dialogue facilitator, for whom really is this notion of peace, and by whom is it really defined? Who truly gets to speak and who is ultimately silenced? When "democratic structures" exist, how does one really ensure that subtle power dynamics do not interfere with the process?

On a larger scale, peace talks and processes among nations' or groups' leaders are often viewed suspiciously when one group appears to have more at stake than another group. For instance, in the case of the Oslo Accords, Said (1996) and other Palestinian scholars questioned the authenticity of these peace talks between Israeli and Palestinian officials from both a historical and contemporary perspective, likening them to nineteenth-century colonial endeavors:

> What it reminds me of is nineteenth century Africa, where European powers would sign pieces of paper called "treaties" with various African chiefs in order that trade and conquest could take place behind a façade of legitimacy, complete with "negotiations" and elaborate ceremonies ... The Arab people certainly want peace and prosperity, but not the humiliating peace imposed on the region by Israel and the US in which a few individuals will profit, whereas the overwhelming majority will either be impoverished or sucked into a merciless economic and social system controlled by transnational corporations and one or two distant powers.
>
> (ibid.: 89)

While some may disagree with the analogy made by Said, this point illustrates a common critique and hesitation that many have towards government-sponsored peace negotiations.

Peace dialogues among 'ordinary' members of civil society, however, are often not met with the same cynicism, at least in mainstream imagination. Discourses surrounding these initiatives generally suggest that the people involved are extraordinary trailblazers, daring to do what their governments or leaders will and cannot. In fact, the mission statement of Seeds of Peace, an encounter program that brings youth together from conflicting sides, states that they are "doing what no government can" (Seeds of Peace, 2009). Moreover, during the height of the Cold War, Samantha Smith, the young

10-year-old North American girl who wrote a letter to Yuri Andopov, became an overnight media sensation and she was named an Ambassador for Peace before her untimely death. While she was not engaging in dialogue groups with her Russian peers, but rather, went to the head of State himself, her role as an ordinary citizen endeavoring peace catapulted her to international stardom.

Despite the aforementioned critiques regarding critical pedagogy and dialogue in education, there is only recently an emerging body of research on the ways power operates among participants in peace education co-existence and encounter programs. These studies have begun to examine the often neglected asymmetries of power that affect the ways in which participants engage in such programs (see Abu-Nimmer, 2004; Moaz, 2000; Ohanyan and Lewis, 2005; Yablon, 2007). Additionally, Gur Ze'ev (2001) has suggested that the project of peace education, like critical pedagogy, is inherently problematic because of its ties to the rational post-Enlightenment thought. In particular, he questions the assumptions that are associated with peace education, including its universal desirability, its necessity, its definition of opposite of war, and argues that in fact, the contemporary discussions on peace education not only serve various violences, but also that "peace education is itself a manifestation of those violences" (ibid.: 315). He locates the origins of peace education in Enlightenment humanist modern ideals and traditions, which ultimately are troubling because of their totalizing and universalizing nature.

Within actual encounter groups, the ways in which participants engage may highlight the ways in which these initiatives function as disciplinary mechanisms. For instance, participants may very well be acutely aware of how particular discourses function to reinscribe power relations among group members, resulting in performances that are concordant with these very same discourses or, perhaps, a disengagement from the actual dialogue group itself. As mentioned earlier, my own observations and experiences as a co-existence facilitator helped shed light on this phenomenon. Yet, the experiences of others regarding the efficacy and role of co-existence groups and peace education in general can also contribute to this analysis. For instance, several students of peace education and conflict resolution have admittedly left their degree programs because they felt notions of privilege and power were not sufficiently problematized in peace education discourse. Another colleague, who worked for two years as a facilitator for youth at an encounter group camp, was frustrated about the choice of English as the medium of dialogue, which ultimately disadvantaged one group over another. She believed that the negligence of how power is inherent in language mirrored the broader power dynamics that took place among the represented groups in general.

The most revelatory discussion, however, was with Suleiman, a Palestinian man who lived in New York City at the time of the interview. Conducted in 2006, before both the summer war between Israel and Hizbollah in Lebanon and the 2008–9 War in Gaza, the analysis of this interview reconsiders the very notion of dialogue to think anew some of the problems and assumptions associated with dialogue work and encounter groups, namely the granting of "equal voice" in group settings when there are existing asymmetrical power relations and dynamics that define the broader context. Moreover, while this perspective is certainly one of many, it is an illustrative partial narrative of how ostensibly harmless concepts, like 'empathy,' can contribute to regulating populations (in this case, who is "humanized" and who is not), as well as show how discourses around one concept (peace) potentially overlap with discourses around other concepts (such as fairness and equality).

While the earlier critiques of critical pedagogy highlight some of the limits of dialogue as an emancipatory tool for social change, Judith Butler's (1990) analysis on the hidden power dynamics among women in dialogue groups are useful to my reading of Suleiman's concerns (and ultimate refusal) to engage in "Israeli/Palestinian" peace dialogues (revealing potential concerns with dialogue groups in general). In her deconstruction of feminist theory that pre-supposes a unitary "women" identity, she asserts that there have been efforts to formulate coalitionist politics through proposing "dialogical encounter by which variously positioned women articulate separate identities within the framework of an emergent coalition" (ibid.: 14). While it is inherent to most encounter groups to assume a more obvious binary structure (i.e. Israeli/Palestinian; Black/White; Christian/Muslim/etc.) to form the dialogue group,[5] its premise is to erode this binary between "enemies" so that they can see their commonalities and move towards peace. Yet, as Butler points out, this orientation towards a particular goal is potentially problematic, as

> despite the clearly democratizing impulse that motivates coalition build-ing, the coalitional theorist can inadvertently reinsert herself as sovereign in the process by trying to assert an ideal form of coalitional structures in advance, one that will effectively guarantee unity as the outcome.
>
> (ibid.: 14)

In other words, the teleological outcome inherent in such dialogical encounters trumps the attempt to create a democratic and equalized forum.

This tendency is evident in my own previously described experience as a practitioner and facilitator in conflict resolution dialogue groups, though the effect on participants may be even more egregiously harmful. Suleiman's refusal to engage in such dialogue groups does not stem from a desire to not want peace, but rather, according to him, is motivated by a means of self-preservation and protection. In the following excerpt, he explains why peace-building as a premise for dialogue is inherently problematic:

> The first problem basically is the word peace ... the word peace has been hijacked by the mainstream American media and their followers ... really distorted to mean some kind of a settlement that ends violence between Israel and the occupied Palestinians. In general, in absolute, I think peace means lack of war, lack of violence, lack of fighting, but it also means

some state of well-being that is based on values and justice and fairness and equality and humanity, etc. ... Otherwise, there is no peace. Peace in the mainstream media means some sort of settlement. The way it is being played out is that a settlement is largely, 99%, to the advantage of Israel, who are the occupying force in this case. What is happening is that the term is being coerced by the media and the argument is being turned against Palestinians. Repeatedly, Israelis keep coming up with unfair settlements, and when the Palestinians do not accept these settlements, they are accused of not wanting to accept peace. The word peace is very offensive in terms of the implication of having to settle with something that is less than fair.

(Interview, May 16, 2006)

In this excerpt, Suleiman actually agrees with many peace education theorists that comprehensive peace is not merely about the absence of war (negative peace), but also about an attainment of equality and social justice (positive peace). His contention with dialogue groups is the emphasis on the word (and outcome of) peace itself, which he articulates embodies a "mainstream" meaning, one that has become equated with unfair settlements and occupation. His take on peace, based on his own experience, might be analogous to how some Iraqis might presently view the term 'democracy' with distrust.

While most peace educators certainly acknowledge how the word 'democracy' has been co-opted to continue war and facilitate one group's interests at the expense of another, there is less critical reflection on how the concept of 'peace' might operate in a similar way. Though Suleiman is specifically placing the concept of peace in a broader context, he then explains how the macro-level political dynamics influence the possibilities of micro-level personal dynamics:

The other thing about peace often the way that it is used in the media is that there are two fighting parties, who have the same opportunities and the same validity of argument. Peace talks, for example, are portrayed to be between two parties of an equally valid claim, which is so far from the truth ... It is like the colonial Americans and the Native Americans sitting around a table and talking about peace after they have been decimated pretty much.

(Interview, May 16, 2006)

In this passage, Suleiman holds the view that notions of peace ignore his perception of asymmetrical power relations among conflicting groups. Though not specifically referencing the role of the 'ordinary person' in peace talks and encounters, he suggests that inherent to the binary set-up of such groups, whether among leaders or civil society, are power dynamics or inequities that remain unacknowledged. The assumption of an equalized or neutral playing field is not only intrinsic to such endeavors, it is also fallacious and insidious.

As a result, Suleiman makes clear why he will not participate in encounter groups:

> So, why would I have a problem being in that room? Because justice has not been done yet. And so I am sitting with the children of privileged people who have occupied my house and stolen my land and killed lots and lots and lots of innocent people. And I am sitting with them and I am giving them a chance to speak up. I actually do not want to give them a chance to speak up. I want justice to be done first. Why would I sit there and watch those people enjoy the fruits of their crimes while taunting me about their fucking prosperity and their fucking privilege and their fucking American accent? And their expensive sneakers and their peace of mind because they live in privilege and sit in this group? Who wants to watch this?
>
> (Interview, May 16, 2006)

Again, Suleiman stresses various inequities between the two groups as a premise for not engaging in dialogue.

Further, he explains that 'justice' might need to happen before 'peace,' or at least before he engages in dialogue. While justice is not necessarily defined in this passage—(one could ask if it is legal rights, compensation, political recognition, the right of return for refugees, etc.)—Suleiman sets this concept as the premise for 'peace talks,' indicating that some form of justice, in a way that seems fair and satisfactory to him, must occur prior to any type of contact among the participants; otherwise, he argues, contact groups are designed to privilege one group over another. For instance, he explains:

> You have to talk to them on an equal footing when you cannot because they have my bicycle [using an analogy that his bicycle has been stolen]. It is impossible for me to be comfortable or constructive unless first they give me my bicycle back and then maybe, but probably not, I might be interested in hearing their perspective, though I have heard it many times and I am sick and tired of hearing it. It is irrelevant to me. The only thing their perspective could do is falsely justify or erroneously justify what they have done. Why would I want to hear their perspective? There is absolutely no perspective possible that could justify what the Israeli government has done. Any possible argument, no matter how painful or tragic, to justify what they have done. Already, I do not think there is any room for me to change my perspective based on what they have said. I could feel sorry for them based on an emotional argument, but do I want to? Absolutely not. It could beef up my general knowledge, so I have more ways to counter back. But the thing that really, really scares me, if you want me to be honest, is that I do not want this experience to humanize them in my eyes.
>
> (Interview, May 16, 2006)

This excerpt has several layers. As earlier, when pushed on the issue of potentially "dialoguing," Suleiman states that for him, the occupation must end first and this notion of justice must be realized. He once again articulates what he believes to be an unacknowledged power differential in the group. He also seems to be stating that one 'side' has had some sort of acknowledgement of the injustices committed against them, while the other 'side,' his side, has not. This contributes to his sense that there are not only larger structural inequalities and disparities between them, but also that there are asymmetries in how each side is perceived globally.

Additionally, Suleiman expresses a fear of 'humanizing,' revealing an interesting and perhaps unexpected response about the unintentional harm of dialogue. While he does not give a full explanation for this fear, one might wonder if it is based on the possibility that empathy will not be reciprocated. He does contend, however, that this expectation of humanization may function to obscure the claims that he has regarding equity and justice. Suleiman later explains how several of his Palestinian friends do engage in such encounter talks with Israelis to make sure that a Palestinian perspective is represented. While he commends them for doing it, he contends, "I do not know how they do it. I just can't. I cannot physically use my body in that way" (Interview, May 16, 2006). For him, the actual physicality of sitting in a dialogue group is painful.

At a later point, upon further reflection, Suleiman expresses that he would participate, or let his child participate in an encounter camp for youth, if in fact, the certain preconditions were met:

> I guess, if you set it up in a way that represents the conflict, and then I would feel better about my kid going. If you set it up from the get go that the Israelis are the children of the occupiers, then you could discuss on that basis. This is the problem that I had with all of the peace talks that the Americans sponsored. This was not stated from the get go that one side is the occupier. It is humiliating for me to sit at the same table as people that are not recognized as occupiers from the get go. It is very offensive … Why should I give them the same right to speak as I do? To influence the observers? They have had 99% of the right already to express their point of view and the Palestinians have had 1%. Look, I have Israelis friends and what allows me to do that is from the get go, they agree that their government did what they did, and they renounce the actions of their governments. That basis set the level for me. Then I can humanize them and love them and talk to them.
>
> (Interview, May 16, 2006)

While he does not use the word justice in this excerpt, he gives more clarity to the preconditions of dialogue by insisting on an acknowledgement of asymmetrical power relations by way that represent the conflict.

DANGEROUS AND THE POLITICS OF IDENTITY: AN
ANALYSIS OF DIALOGUE WORK

Collectively, these excerpts could be read in various ways to reveal the (un) intended consequences of encounter groups as disciplinary mechanisms and producers of harm and violence. One of the first issues that Suleiman raises is the seemingly simple premise of bringing together two 'groups' to share experiences that equalize them in a way so that 'peace' can be achieved. Yet, as Butler asserts:

> Perhaps also part of dialogical understanding entails the acceptance of divergence, breakage, splinter, and fragmentation as part of the often tortuous process of democratization. The very notion of "dialogue" is culturally specific and historically bound, and while one speaker may feel secure that a conversation is happening, another may be sure it is not. The power relations that condition and limit dialogic possibilities need first to be interrogated. Otherwise, the model of dialogue risks relapsing into a liberal model that assumes speaking agents occupy equal positions of power and speak with the same presuppositions about what constitutes "agreement" and "unity" and indeed, that those goals are sought.
>
> (1990: 14–15)

In this case, the words 'agreement' and 'unity' might be interchanged with the ways that these programs use words like 'peace,' 'understanding,' or even 'humanization,' and Suleiman, in his questioning of 'the equal validity claim,' challenges the hope in dialogue and the supposed subsequent foundation for peace. He is vehement in his belief that until there is some sort of 'justice,' the concept of 'peace' will not only serve the interest of the dominant (in this case, Israeli) group, but also serve to render his perspective as 'irrational.' The premise of an encounter group that assumes equal voice for all participants (often by merely having equal numbers from both 'sides') is inherently problematic for him, similar to the issues that Boler (2000) raises about democratic dialogue and power in a multicultural classroom setting.

Moreover, the binary identity structure that is set up as the premise for such encounter groups serves in many ways as a "trap," even for those that are cognizant of the multiple identities that constitute the human subject. For instance, Suleiman, when discussing his resistance to encounter groups, becomes inscribed in fixed discourse about the Israeli/Palestinian binary, despite saying earlier that "there is not one Palestinian group, one side. There are so many Palestinian sides, and each of them serves a different purpose or interest ... there is not one Palestinian cause." He expresses mistrust of Palestinian or any form of nationalism and yet, when discussing the issues on dialogue, he is immediately enmeshed in this binary discourse that he often claims to reject. Perhaps this reveals that even within the rejection of dialogue, one is still compelled to explain his/her disagreement with it within the parameters of the dominant discourse. In this sense, dialogue is highly problematic because it reconstitutes a unified speaker, especially when the constituted speaker ordinarily recognizes his or her partial identity.

Moreover, it could be argued that Suleiman (and others) also become inscribed in the discourses around 'equality' and 'justice,' without ever interrogating how these concepts might also function in the same disciplinary way as the concept of 'peace.' Gur Ze'ev explains that there is a "growing Palestinian demand in Israel to problematize the status quo and challenge this [Israeli hegemonic] order and the kind of peace that it longs for" (2001: 334). However, he also warns that the quest for a 'just peace' may also serve to maintain a hegemonic attitude among Palestinians, one that perpetuates a status quo that solely calls for the complete "abolition of the Zionist project" (ibid.: 334). Thus, while he contends that these types of co-existence programs certainly maintain the Israeli hegemony, he also warns that they contribute to sustaining a static Palestinian narrative as well. This is evident in the ways in which Suleiman evokes a singular Palestinian identity when explaining his objection to dialogue.

Yet, specific to this discussion, Suleiman is also troubling the supposedly humanizing or emancipatory outcome of dialogue and resorts to words like justice to explain how 'peace' might operate to circumvent what he might desire. In fact, when he states that he is really afraid that these types of dialogues might humanize "them," one could also wonder if this fear is based on the potential consequences of not visibly participating (whether performed or not) in the humanization of the "Other." Would he (or his people) be seen as less human if the proper amount of empathy was not demonstrated? If not demonstrating empathy is viewed as 'bad,' 'uncaring,' or even 'evil' in normalizing discourses and behaviors, does a participant truly have a choice to not 'humanize' or empathize with the Other? In this sense, the concepts of empathy and humanization function as disciplinary tools, much in the same way that Foucault's analogy of the panopticon creates and constructs obedient inmates through self-regulation.

Rather than being subject to the normalizing gaze of those in the encounter group and being constructed as a 'bad' person who cannot be sympathetic to the "Other," does opting out of the process altogether allow Suleiman a type of political agency, or act, that would otherwise not be available to him if he participated in the dialogue group? Does couching the conditions for dialogue in terms like 'equality' and 'justice' allow Suleiman to reclaim his own humanity without ever being forced to possible abdicate it (in the eyes of the Other) in a dialogue encounter group?

THE END OF DIALOGUE?: CONCLUDING COMMENTARY

These last questions open up possibilities for those who may feel blighted by what seems like the endless and circular ways in which power relations harm and are reproduced in these processes. It is important to note, however, that while power is pervasive, it is also productive. Foucault explained his stance on this by stating

> not that everything is bad, but that everything is dangerous, which is not exactly the same as bad. If everything is dangerous, then we always have something to do. So my position leads not to apathy but to a hyper- and pessimistic activism.
>
> (1983: 231–32)

Human agency, therefore, is not immobilized by interrogating the ways in which power operates, and is in fact directly related to it.

What, then, are the possibilities in either dialogue work or endeavors for co-existence? Butler (1990) suggests that an acknowledgement of the contradictions of dialogue work is necessary, so that these contradictions are kept intact rather than "resolved." Gur Ze'ev further proposes there is a need "to decipher the material, historical, and political context of normalizing education and challenge it with a counter education that will not be anything other than one more version of normalizing education" (2001: 334). He suggests that this involves a counter-education that is embedded in a "negative utopia" that both resists the "positive utopia of peace education and its universalistic essentialism" and avoids "reintroducing violence as 'justified' counter violence" (ibid.: 335). Like Butler (1990), Gur Ze'ev contends that dialogue must function to recognize its conceptual and historical and situatedness and "never offer peace of mind or symmetrical relations" (2001: 336). Thus, rather than trying to resolve asymmetries or contradictions, the counter-education also implies that these dynamics are interrogated though not resolved.

While a complete abandonment or disengagement from dialogue may appear overly nihilistic, advocates for encounter-based peace education need to reconsider the harmful and inadvertent consequences of (and reasons for) their desire for dialogue, particularly as these encounters may operate to reify re-constituted identities in the name of co-existence. As Jones succinctly states:

> It is undeniable that fantasies and acts of shared communication are preferable to fantasies and acts of ignorance and separation. However, desires for communication must be mediated more by cautious critique and limited expectations than by urgent and ultimately self-defeating optimism.
>
> (2004: 66–67)

At present, it is clear that identity-based encounter programs may potentially cause more damage than intended. One possibility might be to move away from the obsession of creating contrived spaces for inter-group conversation and honor more organically based exchange. In places where the physicality of conflict separates groups, perhaps there should be a shift from solely running face-to-face inter-group encounters towards mono-cultural affinity spaces in which group members can contest, engage, and challenge more freely. Though power may also operate in these exchanges similarly to the way that it does in encounter groups, we should also be reminded that any attachment to a specific idealistic vision is potentially dangerous.

Notes

1 Examples of this might be when a participant exemplified empathy for the 'other' or when one changed from a hard-line position to a more 'tolerant' one.
2 Foucault's seminal piece, Discipline and Punish (1979), examines how power operates pervasively to regulate the mind, body, and soul of the individual.
3 Critical pedagogy builds upon concepts of the Frankfurt School negative critique, Gramscian hegemony and counter-hegemony, and Freirean critical consciousness (see Hantzopoulos, 2008).
4 Negative peace is the absence of direct organized physical violence and positive peace is the absence of structured violence and a commitment to social justice and human rights (see Galtung, 1969; Harris and Morrison, 2003; Reardon, 2000).
5 In some cases, encounter groups may focus on several identities (such as Serbian, Croat, Bosnian). The idea is that as with binary structures, the identities are somewhat fixed rather than dynamic.

References

Abu-Nimmer, M. (2002). "Israeli-Palestinian Dialogue in the Second Intifada: Between Despair and Hope," Global Dialogue, 4(3), 130–43.
——(2004). "Education for Co-existence and Arab-Jewish Encounters in Israel: Potential and Challenges," Journal of Social Issues, 60(2), 405–22.
Amnesty International (2009). "Report," available at: http://thereport.amnesty.org/ press-area/en/irene-khans-speech (accessed July 22, 2009).
Bajaj, M. (2008). "Introduction," in M. Bajaj (Ed.), *The Encyclopedia of Peace Education*. Charlotte, NC: Information Age Publishing, pp. 1–9.
Bar-Tal, D. (2000). "From Intractable Conflict Through Conflict Resolution to Reconciliation: Psychological Analysis," Political Psychology, 21, 351–65.
——(2002). "The Elusive Nature of Peace Education," in G. Salomon and B. Nevo (Eds.), *Peace Education: The concept, principles and practice in the world*. Mahwah, NJ: Lawrence Erlbaum, pp. 27–36.
——(2004). "Nature, Rationale, and Effectiveness of Education for Co-Existence," Journal of Social Issues, 60(2), 253–71.
Bartlett, L. (2005). "Dialogue, Knowledge, and Teacher-Student Relations: Freirean Pedagogy in Theory and Practice," Comparative Education Review, 49(3), 1–21.
——(2009). *The Word and the World: The cultural politics of literacy in Brazil*. Creskill, NJ: Hampton Press.
Basu, R. (1997). "Geosurveillance Through the Mapping of Test Results: An Ethical Dilemma or Public Policy Solution?," ACME: An International E-Journal for Critical Geographies, 3(2), 87–111.
Boler, M. (2000). "All Speech Is Not Free: The Ethics of 'Affirmative Action Pedagogy,'" in L. Stone (Ed.), *Philosophy of Education Yearbook*. Urbana, IL: Philosophy of Education Society, pp. 321–29.

Butler, J. (1990). *Gender Trouble: Feminism and the subversion of identity*. New York: Routledge.

Dahl, T. (2009). "The Importance of Place for Learning about Peace: Residential Summer Camps as Transformative Thinking Spaces," Journal of Peace Education, 6(2), 225–45.

Danesh, H. B. (2006). "Towards an Integrative Theory of Peace Education," Journal of Peace Education, 3(1), 55–78.

The Economist. (2007). "Still Campaigning for Co-existence," September 1.

Ellsworth, E. (1989). "Why Doesn't This Feel Empowering? Working Through Repressive Myths of Critical Pedagogy," Harvard Educational Review, 59(3), 297–324.

Feuerverger, G. (2001). *Oasis of Dreams: Teaching and learning peace in a Jewish-Palestinian village in Israel*. New York: Routledge/Falmer.

Foucault, M. (1979). *Discipline and Punish*. New York: Vintage Books.

——(1983). "On the Genealogy of Ethics," in H. Dreyfus and P. Rabinow (Eds.), *Michel Foucault: Beyond structuralism and hermeneutics*. Chicago: The University of Chicago Press, pp. 231–32.

Freire, P. (1972/1994). *The Pedagogy of the Oppressed*. New York: Continuum.

Galtung, J. (1969). " Violence, Peace and Peace Research," Journal of Peace Research, 6, 167–91.

Gore, J. (1992). "What Can We Do for You! What Can 'We' Do for 'You'? Struggling over Empowerment in Critical and Feminist Pedagogy," in J. Gore and C. Luke (Eds.), *Feminisms and Pedagogies*. New York: Routledge, pp. 54–73.

Groff, L. (2002). "A holistic view of peace education," Social Alternatives, 21(1), 7–10.

Gur Ze'ev, I. (2001). "Philosophy of Peace Education in a Post-modern Era," Educational Theory, 51(3), 315–36.

Hantzopoulos, M. (2008). "Sizing up Small: An Ethnographic Case Study of a Critical Small High School in New York City,"unpublished dissertation.

Harris, I. (2004). "Peace Education Theory," Journal of Peace Education, 1(1), 5–20.

Harris, I. and Morrison, M. (2003). *Peace Education* (2nd ed.). Jefferson, NC: McFarland.

Jones, A. (2004). "Talking Cure: The Desire for Dialogue," in M. Boler (Ed.), *Democratic Dialogue in Education: Troubling speech, disturbing silence*. New York: P. Lang, pp. 57–67.

Kohl, H. (2009). "The Educational Panopticon," Teachers College Record, available at: http://www.tcrecord.org.

Luke, C. (1992). "Feminist Politics as Radical Pedagogy," in J. Gore and C. Luke (Eds.), *Feminisms and Pedagogies*. New York: Routledge, pp. 25–53.

Moaz, I. (2000). "Multiple Conflicts and Competing Agendas: A Framework for Conceptualizing Structural Encounters between Groups in Conflict: The Case of a Coexistence Project of Jews and Palestinians in Israel," Peace and Conflict: Journal of Peace Psychology, 6, 135–56.

Ohanyan, A. and Lewis, J. (2005). "Politics of Peace-Building: Critical Evaluation of Interethnic Contact Peace Education in Georgian-Peace Camp, 1998–2002," Peace and Change, 30(1), 57–84.

Popkewitz, T. (1998). *Struggling for the Soul: The politics of schooling and the construction of the teacher*. New York: Teachers College Press.

Reardon, B. (1988). *Comprehensive Peace Education*. New York: Teachers College Press.

——(2000). "Peace Education: A Review and Projection," in B. Moon, M. Ben-Peretz, and S. Brown (Eds.), *International Companion to Education*. New York: Routledge, pp. 397–425.

——(2001). "Global Problems as Obstacles to a Culture of Peace," in *Education for a Culture of Peace in a Gender Perspective*. Paris: UNESCO, pp. 111–33).

Rouhana, N. N., and Korper, S. H. (1997). "Power Asymmetry and Goals of Unofficial Third Party Intervention in Protracted Intergroup Conflict," Journal of Peace Psychology, 3, 1–17.

Said, E. (1996). *Peace and Its Discontents: Essays on Palestine in the Middle East peace process*. New York: Vintage.

Salomon, G. (2002). "The Nature of Peace Education: Not All Programs Are Created Equal," in G. Salomon and B. Nevo (Eds.), *Peace Education: The concepts, principles, and practices around the world*. Mahwah, NJ: Erlbaum, pp. 3–14.

Schimmel, N. (2009). "Towards a Sustainable and Holistic Model of Peace Education: A Critique of Conventional Modes of Peace Education through Dialogue in Israel," Journal of Peace Education, 6(1), 51–68.

Schugurensky, D. (1998). "The Legacy of Paulo Freire: A Critical Review of his Contributions," Convergence: International Journal of Adult Education, 31(1 and 2), 17–29.

Seeds of Peace (2009). "Mission Statement." Available at: www.seedsofpeace.org (accessed June 12, 2009).

Toh, S. H. (2006). "Education for Sustainable Development and the Weaving of a Culture of Peace: Complementaries and Synergies," paper presented at the UNESCO Expert Meeting on Education for Sustainable Development (ESD), Kanchanaburi, Thailand.

Yablon, Y. B. (2007). "Contact Intervention Programs for Peace Education and the Reality of Dynamic Conflicts," Teachers College Record, 109(4), 991–1012.

3 A Grassroots Peace Education Innovation in a Co-operative Jewish-Palestinian Village in Israel

Mahatma Gandhi's Concept of "Satyagraha" in Action

Grace Feuerverger

Do not be daunted by the enormity of the world's grief. Do justly, now. Love mercy, now. Walk humbly, now. You are not obligated to complete the work, but neither are you free to abandon it.

(The Talmud)

A "ZONE OF PEACE"

Mahatma Gandhi's famous words "Be the change you want to see in the world" are embodied in a co-operative community in Israel where Jewish and Palestinian families live together in peaceful co-existence. One dimension of Gandhi's "zone of peace" within his concept of "Satyagraha" is in the non-violent struggle for social justice which he considers as first and foremost a moral imperative and that which is the true purpose of education. How delighted Mahatma Gandhi would have been to witness this little village of Neve Shalom/Wahat Al-Salam. His words are with them every day and are discussed in the village schools; both the elementary school where Jewish and Arab children study together in the same classrooms with both Jewish and Arab teachers leading the classes; and in the conflict resolution program "The School for Peace" which brings together Israeli and Palestinian high-school students from all over Israel and from the occupied territories offering them an opportunity to meet for the first time.

The goal is to create a social, cultural and political framework of equality and mutual respect in which the residents maintain their own cultural heritage, religion, language, and identity. Their philosophy of a Jewish-Arab village in Israel living and teaching peace and equality is rooted in the democratic ideals of discussion and co-operative problem-solving. This chapter is based on a nine-year study that I carried out as ethnographer in this extraordinary village and it is about hope in the midst of deadly conflict (Feuerverger, 2001b). A major focus of this research inquiry is the bilingual/bicultural elementary school as a moral endeavor dedicated to peaceful co-existence, which is coordinated by a teaching team of Jewish and Arab educators, some of whom are residents of the village and some of whom live in neighboring villages. In this chapter I explore those interactions among the students, teachers and parents, emanating from their sense of shared purpose which reflects their assumptions about the nature of education in their village and about the type of society they wish to promote through education. The school attempts to foster cooperation and mutual respect for its students of Muslim, Christian and Jewish backgrounds. I share narrative portraits of some remarkable teachers, students and parents in a learning environment that could potentially provide a new and global dimension for exploring moral issues within the context of intercultural and interfaith understanding and conflict resolution.

This chapter is devoted to the complexity and aesthetic of peace education taking place in the classrooms of an elementary school in a village where Jews and Palestinians are involved in peaceful co-existence both personally and professionally. In this chapter I provide a reflective analysis of the interviews carried out with the teachers and students in the elementary school in the village. My aim is to focus on meaning-making as grounded in personal life history—that is, on the social, linguistic and cultural stories of my participants (and of myself) in an attempt at a more nuanced view of peacemaking in education. Their philosophy of a Jewish-Arab village in Israel, living and teaching peace and equality, is rooted in the democratic ideals of dialogue and co-operative problem-solving. But it is not as simple and utopian as that. It is a "flesh-and-blood" place within a very difficult human circumstance where inter-group conflict in the wider society and the moral problems and dilemmas that ensue are constantly being played out and negotiated. The village is not an island unto itself by any means. Many of the villagers work in towns nearby, and are subject to the social and political turmoil that envelops all of Israel (see Feuerverger, 1995, 1997, 2001a). Effective schools should be sites of political and cultural negotiation which encourage teachers to situate and scrutinize the borders of their own ideological discourses. "Borders elicit a recognition of those epistemological, political, cultural and social margins that define 'the places that are safe and unsafe, [that] distinguish us from them'" (Anzaldua, 1987). Teachers need to become cognizant of the "unconscious myths" that have shaped the mental and physical landscape of their lives and which now motivate them in the planning of curriculum and in their choice of interpersonal classroom strategies (Richardson, 1994; Clandinin and Connelly, 1995). The conversations I had with the teachers and students in this school were very illuminating in terms of language, culture and identity formation.

THEORETICAL FRAMEWORK

One of the greatest challenges in Israeli society is to overcome the fear and enmity that have evolved through the years of war between Jew and Arab. One of the Jewish parents very eloquently expressed her hope which is shared by all those connected with the school: "We want our children to learn in friendship and joy, not in conflict and sorrow." In order to make friends with "the other," as the residents in this village are doing, we must confront the "other" in the deepest part of our souls, in the psychological no-man's land where the 'foreigner' lurks—"he is the hidden face of our identity, the space that wrecks our abode, the time in which understanding and affinity founder"(Kristeva, 1991). In this qualitative study, I examine how the participants acknowledge that 'foreigner' who speaks a different language and has a different culture and different values and traditions and who competes for the same geo-political space. This is an excruciating task but when it is embarked upon, it opens up the possibility of collaboration instead of competition and hostility, and in so doing it surmounts the hegemonic discourses and institutions and thereby creates transformative inter-group and inter-personal dialogues. Van Manen (1990) explains that "we gather other people's experiences because they allow us to become more experienced ourselves." Connelly and Clandinin (1990) support this view and claim that narrative refers to the process of making meaning of experience by telling stories of personal and social relevance.

Although there has been substantial research on various aspects of language, identity and intercultural relations in many parts of the world, there has been very little work on the specific consequences of bilingual/bicultural programs in which children from majority and minority groups learn together against a larger backdrop of conflict and war with the ultimate goal of peaceful co-existence. There is very little qualitative research that focuses on a social grouping in which the residents are actively dedicated to issues of peacemaking in their daily lives. This chapter intends to explore the social and psychological complexities of moral development through this specific educational experience. "Moral experience" here will refer to the "lived experience" (see Dilthey, 1910/1977, cited in Tappan and Brown, 1989; Bakhtin, 1986) of my participants as they are confronted with everyday situations filled with moral conflicts, ambiguities, and dilemmas. I focus on giving meaning to their "lived experiences" by presenting them in narrative form. There is a growing understanding in the research literature of narrative as a powerful way of giving meaning to human life experiences (see, for example, Geertz, 1988; Gilligan, 1982;Noddings, 1991, 2003; Pinar, 1988; Polkinghorne, 1988; Sarbin, 1986). This theoretical approach is congruent with Gilligan's focus on the analysis of moral voice and development by using narrative as a vehicle to examine conflicts and their possible resolution in interpersonal relationships (in Tappan and Brown, 1989: 199). Tappan and Brown (ibid.: 182) note that narrative is central to the study of, as well as to the teaching of morality, and that authorship of moral choices, actions and feelings develops a sense of moral sensibility. Indeed, the deepening crisis in American schools and society (see Kozol, 1991) is obliging educators to explore educational programs that encourage moral development in its students through narrative. This study offers a narrative of what can be termed a grassroots, organic peace education initiative and involves personal and professional accounts of teachers' and students' lives in terms of moral educational issues.

AN INTERACTIVE METHODOLOGY

One of the major aims of this study is to give the participants a voice and to construct meaning for their texts. I searched for the patterns and narrative threads that would bring together their lived experiences into a collective story. As participant-observer, I was concerned with the interaction between personal life histories and the shaping of assumptions about the teaching-learning experience in relation to cultural and linguistic diversity, indeed, to a situation of conflict between two peoples in a land which they must learn to share. This inquiry was based on a strong interactive relationship between myself and my participants through dialogue and conversation. The research approach for this study therefore involved a variety of qualitative methodologies. Case study and narrative methodologies were adopted in order to document the construction and reconstruction of the meaning of teaching and learning from a moral perspective for the individual teachers, students and parents (see Kohlberg, 1985) in the specific bilingual/bicultural school setting of the village of Neve Shalom/Wahat Al-Salam (see Connelly and Clandinin, 1990, 1995; Eisner and Peshkin, 1990; Huberman and Miles, 1984; Yin, 1984). I therefore chose a narrative approach in order to give voice to the moral/educational initiatives that these villagers are creating. Carol Witherell (1991; Witherall and Noddings, 1999) states that we "as educators are inescapably involved in the formation of moral communities as well as the shaping of persons" (Witherell, 1991: 239) and I highlight the phrase Maxine Greene (2000) adapted from Toni Morrison's novel Beloved (1987) to say that "moral education requires becoming friends of one another's minds, even, perhaps especially, when the other is 'stranger'"(see Witherell, 1991: 238–39). In this process, all participants were encouraged to reflect on their own personal philosophy on intergroup relations vis-à-vis the teaching and learning experience. Indeed, ethnographic and narrative research methodology was required here because of its emphasis on "thick" description, on process, and on the natural setting (i.e. the classroom, the home, the village) as the source of data (see, for example, Janesick, 1991).

Through the vehicle of narrative and reflexive ethnographic methodology, I try to make sense of the personal as well as professional experiences of my participants in their quest for intercultural harmony. Finally, within the theoretical framework of this study, the specific educational initiative of this school as a "moral community" provides a window through which the issues of schools' relationships to multicultural and multiracial communities can be observed and elucidated more generally in a global context. I documented the experiences of the children and teachers through in-depth interviews and participant-observation in the school, and through a general "reflection-in-living" (see Schön, 1991) within the village. The interviews were unstructured and as open-ended as possible. Students and teachers shared with me their stories about why they decided to live in this village; about the dreams that they had for the children's future; about their great satisfaction with the school; and about the fragile sense of hope they nurtured for peace in their troubled land.

MORAL DEVELOPMENT THROUGH NARRATIVES OF LIVED EXPERIENCES

The discussion in this chapter has two levels of discourse. First, it reflects my impressions of the village and the school, both the physical and psychological surroundings. Furthermore, it explores the process of narrating stories of moral development and thereby authoring one's moral lived experiences and ultimately taking responsibility for action. There are a number of meta-themes that I explore in the narrative structure of this study. They are: (1) the commitment of the participants to confront the central question of Jewish-Arab peaceful co-existence on a grassroots level within the village and school; (2) the school as a micro-society and as a moral community that can be used as a role model for conflict resolution and peacemaking; and (3) the village as a symbol for creating a dialogue between Arabs and Jews in the larger Israeli society: negotiation and compromise in an atmosphere of moral dilemma and goodwill.

I cannot help but think that Robert Coles was discussing my own reflexive ethnographic "gaze" when he wrote:

> To some extent we see the world we are looking for. We select for ourselves visually what our minds and hearts crave to notice ... How differently each of us sees even the same scene, selecting from it what we want to emphasize out of our personal needs and nature.
>
> (1989: 224–25)

Perhaps I, as a child of Holocaust survivors, a "border-dweller," have been searching for Neve Shalom/Wahat Al-Salam all my life and finally found it. As a child, I longed to live in a world of harmony and joy and peace. I agree with Britzman (1998) that my own telling is fragmented and dominated by the "discourses of my time and place" and especially by my sense of being a border-dweller, someone still searching for 'home'. I confess openly to this guilty desire. Perhaps we must indeed acknowledge ethnography as a "regulating fiction, as a particular narrative practice that produces textual identities and regimes of truth" (ibid: 236).

Craig Kridel underscores the "power of autobiography and biography—the construction of landscapes and the act of making history personal" (1998: 122). Indeed, Denzin and Lincoln (1995) suggest that the means for interpretive, ethnographic practices are still not clear, but it is certain that things will never be the same. We are in a new age where messy, uncertain, multi-voiced texts, cultural criticism, and new experimental works will become more common, as will more reflexive forms of fieldwork, analysis, and intertextual representation.

(ibid.: 15, as cited in Kridel, 1998)

Renato Rosaldo (1989/1993) contends that there are no "innocent" ethnographers. There is always an interior voice crying to be heard; to be acknowledged; to be recognized within the exterior professional world. We are all moved by deep unconscious forces, and that is nothing if not human. The multiple layerings that become the foundation upon which we do our "formal" ethnographic work emerge from personal, private experiences and ways of knowing (Belenky et al., 1986)—which are not incongruent with theoretical, epistemological frames of reference. In fact, the fragments have in themselves a certain coherence, a raw clarity of purpose: they represent the emotional chaos—the landscapes of loss, of pain, of fear, of trauma that create the underpinnings of this struggle towards peace which I became intimately involved. The stuff of ethnography, indeed perhaps of all human endeavour, is in the endless retellings and thus in illuminating the enormous questions located in the vicissitudes and incredible contradictions of human relationships, the "us" versus "them" dichotomies. This little village reminds me of Martin Buber's eloquent description of the "narrow ridge is the place where I and Thou meet": the territory of the between where people can come together in community; what Paul Tillich called The Courage to Be (as cited in Palmer 1988: 59). I write with a longing that I believe we all share: to reclaim the lost garden of Eden where peace reigned. Will we be forever in exile in a no-man's land between faith and despair? Whatever knowledge is it begins in that place of longing deep within the soul. Perhaps that is the price we must pay for seeking knowledge, for seeking truth. As educators, as academics; indeed as human beings working for social justice in the world we have no choice but to walk that difficult and often lonely path. It is like a prayer. And in the grim realization of how much suffering continues to haunt so many inhabitants of this planet we must find a way back to that innocent love which we knew in some far-off land of our dreams. I share here some pieces of stories that my participants offered and it is in writing them down on paper (or rather on the screen) that I discover some comfort and some strength to keep going in the shadow of this journey. I write down their stories in the hope that you the reader are willing to take risks along with my participants and myself and to find some direction out of the confusion of conflict.

In the following section, I offer excerpts of the in-depth interviews which I conducted with students and teachers both formally and informally, as well as reflections of my classroom observations, in order to explore the discourses of peace and conflict resolution within curriculum development, pedagogical strategies and interpersonal communication at Neve Shalom/Wahat Al-Salam.

These data were tape-recorded and later transcribed. The methodological tools of fieldnote gathering and journaling were always central to this inquiry and were kept on a daily basis.

I begin with Yusef, the co-director of the school who explained how language awareness has offered a new pedagogical and social paradigm for the Jewish and Arab children:

> In this school, Arabic and Hebrew both hold prominent positions and the children are fully aware of that in all classroom activities. Because each class has an Arab and a Jewish teacher, the children are exposed to two points of view. For example, I teach Actualia (current events) with a Jewish teacher and we are able to discuss difficult, controversial issues immediately with our pupils. Language is such a key point here. Let's face it, learning the history of Israel in Hebrew is totally different from learning it in Arabic! Learning its history in both languages is the beginning of a whole new future. This is radical stuff! The Israeli War of Independence has a totally different connotation in Arabic and that awareness that we teachers can offer them, opens new doors for these young people.

Yusef is in effect agreeing with many researchers who claim that language is the essential means by which teachers shape their experience and explain the world to themselves and also to their students. This participant went on to explain how he struggled to become not only fluent in Hebrew but also to excel in Hebrew literature at the Hebrew University in Jerusalem which was quite unusual for an Arab in the early 1970s and even today. I asked him what motivated him to pursue this course of study. He replied:

> To become a student in Hebrew literature meant I could conquer my insecurities about being an Arab minority person in Israel. It gave me a sense of confidence that changed my life and eventually brought me to this place in order that I can help other Arab students to overcome their inferiority feelings. It's all about language, identity and power. Using both languages is a symbol of co-existence and the possibility of friendship. And gives me a sense of equality with Jewish-Israelis.

Yusef discussed at length his frustration about living in the "space between borders"; where he had no sense of belonging either to his Israeli self nor to his Palestinian self. He, like Palestinian-Israeli author Anton Shammas who writes in Hebrew not Arabic, is "in the space of exile at home ... exile from a homeland that no longer exists except in nostalgia and ideological space." "By writing in Hebrew, the language of his conquerors," Potok (1988: 298) observes, "the Arab Shammas can realize Derrida's ideal of speaking the other's language without renouncing one's own." These words embody those of Maxine Greene (2000): "For a man who no longer has a homeland, writing becomes a place to live." Lavie (1992) suggests that "these are individuals who must continually remap their border zones so that they can maintain their exilic home in the claimed homeland of the Jews" (quoted in Potok, 1988: 305).

The theme of cultural dislocation and fractured identity underlies the ambivalence that so many Palestinian-Israelis experience in their everyday lives and is evident in the asymmetry of status between Hebrew and Arabic in Israel. Therefore the original attempt at Neve Shalom/Wahat Al-Salam to teach both Hebrew and Arabic in the school curriculum in the early 1980s was more than just an interesting pedagogical idea; it was and still is in essence a powerfully subversive act. This community decision mirrors the powerful force and agency of those Palestinian-Israeli writers who write about their own lived experience in new literary forms and specifically in Hebrew, thus creating alternative norms and value systems. The pedagogy in the school at Neve Shalom/Wahat Al-Salam can thus be regarded as a political act of resistance as well as an act of self-empowerment and carries within it the kind of critical language awareness that liberates.

Indeed, Palestinian author Anton Shammas, on a visit to the village in 1992, used these eloquent words to describe its pedagogy and peace educational commitment: "It is always risky to be lured by metaphors, especially in the Middle East, but those who live in this 'Oasis of Peace' have managed to achieve the impossible: by refusing to be lured, they have concretized a metaphor. We, who are still wandering in the desert, envy them" (from the village newsletter). He speaks of his feelings in terms of language awareness: "At the age of eighteen I chose what I had no choice but to choose: namely to regard Hebrew as my stepmother tongue. Sometimes I feel that this was an act of cultural trespass, and that the day may come when I shall have to account for it" (as quoted in Shipler, 1986: 455).

A Palestinian teacher in the school discussed the surprise that his father showed when he first came to visit his son in this village and met some of the children in the school:

> My father grew up in a little Arab village in the north of the country and was at first uncertain about why I should teach in a school where Jewish and Arab kids were together. He just wasn't sure how this would work. Then on the first afternoon that he was here a little nine year old girl came up to him and spoke to him in Arabic. They had a lovely conversation and afterwards I told him this young student of mine was Jewish. He had assumed she was an Arab because her Arabic was so fluent. When he heard she was Jewish, his eyes filled with tears and he said he thought he would never see this. He was amazed at how all the children were getting along, jumping back and forth into Hebrew and Arabic. They were friends, and that was a revelation to him. That is the beauty of this place.

As participant-observer in this school, I came to recognize that knowing the existence of the 'foreigner', as Kristeva puts it, is a central aspect of language awareness which I believe can be defined as a sensitivity and a conscious understanding of the myriad languages and cultures in our world and of their role for humanity. This study has helped me to understand more fully the dialectical relationship between language and thought in practical educational settings (see for example, Bakhtin, 1981; Dewey, 1938; Vygotsky, 1962). As discussed earlier, I have been involved in multilingual education both personally and professionally as far back as I remember, and I believe that the bilingual (multilingual) classroom must be a space where dialogue is seen as a necessary way to relate authentically to one another through collaboration, reflection, expression (Kaiser and Short, 1998).

A Jewish grade five teacher in the school confided in me:

> I never had the opportunity as a child to learn Arabic the way the Jewish children do here. And only now do I truly realize how it changes everything to simply be able to speak to one another in both languages. It really changes things; it's very symbolic. And the children are unconsciously very aware of this, I think. I will give you a concrete example. A new child came into my class from [a nearby Jewish village] and she did not know Arabic and stayed away from the Arab children. As time went on, she of course began to interact with the Arab children and she began to learn Arabic. It was wonderful to see how her attitude changed in such a positive way. The very same is true for the Arab children who come to this school and begin to learn Hebrew and become friends with the Jewish kids.

A grade six boy from a Jewish village stated why he enjoyed learning both languages at the school:

> I feel very different now that I can speak and read and write Arabic. I didn't have much to do with Arab kids before coming to this school and I was afraid of them because of all the terrorist things. But now I'm making friends with them and I can read stories about their lives and their heroes and their culture and it makes me understand them more and feel closer to them.

This kind of thoughtful teaching and learning is a transformative process which appreciates the complexities of bilingual and bicultural education within a landscape of conflict and war. It embodies the late Paulo Freire's (1970: 75) revolutionary perspective of social liberation in his assertion: "There is no true word that is not at the same time a praxis (action-reflection). Thus to speak of a true word is to transform the world." Indeed, I had the opportunity to observe the dynamics of meaning making through language and cultural awareness, which was grounded in reflective practice. This is what shapes the pedagogical landscape of Neve Shalom/Wahat al-Salam. Knowing that one must learn to co-exist with "the other" is already a form of action; and naming the challenge is a way of overcoming it. The signature discourses of conflict resolution in each classroom underscore their fundamental commitment to peacemaking.

For example, in the weeks that I spent in the school during one of my sojourns in the village, one bulletin board was dedicated to a project about the city of Jerusalem from the different religious and cultural perspectives. Linguistically, the symbols of peace were evident in the textual material that accompanied the various drawings. The Al-Aqsa Mosque was described in Arabic; the Western Wall had a text in Hebrew explaining its significance; and the Church of the Holy Sepulchre was discussed in Arabic. In the center of the wall display was a large story narrating the long and tumultuous history of Jerusalem in both languages. It seemed to me as the observer, that the use of both languages in the story was a salient symbol of peace and it authentically explained that each child is taught to understand their culture and also learn about the other's culture. The drawings with their individual language texts indicate that the goal is co-existence, respect and friendship, but not assimilation. Religion is taught separately, but there are also joint discussions. What is essential, I was told, is that no one is appropriating each other's history or religion or culture. However, when possible, shared narrative accounts are created.

During my many classroom visits, I watched a constant effort at moral negotiation and dialogue for curriculum development within the differential socio-historic and geo-political narratives of that particular moment in history. Benvenisti quoted the famous Israeli author A.B. Yehoshua to indicate the difficulties therein: "History is potent, it has direction and it has meaning" (1995: 154). The tension around these issues was authentically and sensitively dealt with in classrooms, in the staff room and in the playground.

One Hebrew literature teacher discusses the difficulties in creating curriculum that honors the perspectives of both peoples in its textual material:

> When the children learn Hebrew and Arabic it is crucial that they are exposed to narrative texts that open their eyes to the realities of the conflicts between their cultural groups. They need accurate, authentic accounts in their language classes as well as all across the curriculum. In fact each teacher teaches his or her subjects in their own language. The children are exposed to both languages right from the beginning of their schooling. For each subject matter, time is set aside for vocabulary and grammar. It is a great challenge for the Hebrew- and Arabic-speaking teachers to provide pedagogy and materials that are linguistically and conceptually appropriate in meaningful contexts. We have had very tough moments of discord and loud debate in this work, because we do not sweep things under the carpet, and therefore we touch very painful and often unresolvable issues. But we go on, knowing that it is better to acknowledge the problems than to avoid them. And I think in the end only that kind of honesty makes learning possible.

Furthermore, I observed a great deal of peer tutoring between older and younger students, both Arab and Jewish students, helping each other with subject matter on the common ground of each other's language and culture. I was impressed by the power created in their collaborative learning and sharing of knowledge which is encouraged by the school's emphasis on acknowledging the children as experts in their own literacy development. There are various different writing activities: writing on personal subjects (i.e. journal writing) as well as general class writing, and small-group cooperative writing ventures that are often presented to the class as a whole.

This kind of pedagogy creates a place where identities are constructed and is based on the belief that language learning takes place within a setting of authentic learning contexts, that comes directly from the experiences of the children. For example, I recall the activities in a grade one class where the children, guided by their teacher who was a vivacious young Arab woman from a nearby village, were crafting themes revolving around war and loss and a hope for peace and normalcy. Hebrew and Arabic were being used simultaneously and their discussions reflected the actual experiences of their everyday lives. Their "ownership" of the curriculum by the students was evident in this class, as it was in all the classes that I visited. This approach is in keeping with Byram's (1993) proposal for a model of language teaching for cultural awareness that combines both experiential and reflective learning allowing for a greater degree of abstraction and critical analysis (See also Feuerverger, 1995; Gumperz, 1977; Heath, 1983; Nieto, 1992; Tabachnick and Zeichner, 1993).

The teachers whom I interviewed suggest that the intersection between education, language and society cannot be ignored. Teaching and learning are dialogic in nature and Freire talks about dialogic action as an awareness of oneself as "knower," an attitude which he named conscientização. This critical consciousness is informed by his philosophy of language and inspired by his respect for humanity. The villagers at Neve Shalom/Wahat Al-Salam embody Freire's focus on the discursive power of language which brings them to the heart of Freire's pedagogy of knowing: that "naming the world becomes a model for changing the world" (Freire and Macedo, 1987: xv). They are practicing an emancipatory theory of bilingual literacy by developing an alternative educational discourse and reclaiming authorship of their own national identities. Indeed, Freire suggests that

> schools should never impose absolute certainties on students. They should stimulate the certainty of never being too certain—a method vital to critical pedagogy. Educators should also stimulate the possibilities of expression, the possibilities of subjectivity. They should challenge students to "discourse about the world."
>
> (ibid.: 57)

My participants also reinforce Giroux's assertion that:

> The pedagogical should be made more political and the political more pedagogical. In other words, there is a dire need to develop pedagogical practices, in the first instance, that brings teachers, parents and students together around new and more emancipatory visions of community ... that the present as always a time of possibility.
>
> (1991: 6)

The simplest way of telling a story is in the voice of the storyteller. I feel fortunate that these participants opened their hearts and minds to me in the telling of their personal and professional stories. These were honest and authentic encounters—spaces were created where vulnerable feelings were shared in the safety of the conversations. The act of remembering, the act of narrating and listening to retrospective reflection were all braided together into a melange of past experience of marginality and present quest for equality. It enhanced my own reflection on the issue of minority language learning and Jewish-Palestinian relations in a new way. "This self-understanding—which emerges out of the intersubjective experiences of relationships—becomes the impetus for deep inquiry and the construction of knowledge ... In the dynamic mutuality of the relationship," I as the researcher tried to shape, as Lawrence-Lightfoot (Lawrence-Lightfoot and Hoffman Davis, 1997: 152) puts it: "the intellectual and emotional meanings that emerged," all the while being cognizant of my responsibility to "define the boundaries and protect the vulnerability and exposure of the actor." Most importantly, there was a sense of reciprocity in these conversations, which, I believe, showed commitment and legitimacy to what was being said. What also strikes me about the conversations is the power of their educational dream: their imaginings and longings for a school and a society that offer something truly different, truly aesthetically and morally appealing. They are, to my mind, artists in their search for beauty and truth and social justice. Deborah Britzman describes artists as those

> who still worry about this thing called pedagogy, about what it means to teach and to learn, and about the detours known as history ... We have artists unafraid to imagine differences within, to address those who may or may not understand, to fashion communities yet to become, and to engage life at its most incomplete. Unlike [the more usual] educators ... they are interested in the mistakes, the accidents, the detours, and the unintelligibilities of identities ... They gesture to their own constructed-ness and frailties, troubling the space between representation and the real.
>
> (1998: 105)

This eloquent description of the "artist" is indeed congruent with the kind of educators who teach at Neve Shalom/Wahat Al-Salam. These teachers are not afraid to face their relationship to the "other," to their own experience and hence to negotiate the interplay between identity, language and cultural differences. They look within their own village school and within themselves for strategies of negotiation as well as seek conceptual guidance from professional and academic sources from outside. All face the issues of desire and loss as they develop curriculum. It is a question of belonging—to retrieve that which has been expropriated emotionally. Thus they continue to push the limits in their dynamic interaction and to struggle for greater voice as they reach higher and higher and dig deeper and deeper in their community building and social transformation.

I firmly believe that one of the most important contributions we can make as academics is to use the vehicle of our research work as a means of forwarding the cause of peace and equality within an anti-racist/multicultural, multilingual educational context for all societies and to unequivocally support an inclusive curriculum wherein all forms of oppression can be addressed with compassion. Ultimately educational and all forms of human reform are dependent on the importance and power of love: I cite here Freire's universalist message:

> Dialogue cannot exist, however, in the absence of a profound love for the world and for people ... Because love is an act of courage, not of fear, love is commitment to others. No matter where the oppressed are found, the act of love is commitment to their cause—the cause of liberation ... As an act of bravery, love cannot be sentimental: as an act of freedom it must nor serve as a pretext for manipulation. It must generate other acts of freedom; otherwise, it is not love.
>
> (1970: 70–71)

I am comforted and empowered by the philosophy of Freire and in the knowledge/belief systems of mindful, compassionate scholars everywhere who stress that "cultural workers must create alliances across national borders ... and that, in Freirian terms, revolutionary love is always pointed in the direction of commitment and fidelity to a global project of emancipation" (McLaren, 1999: 53–54).

CONCLUDING REMARKS

From its very beginning, this inquiry became a shared experience which intended to validate all participants (including myself as researcher) and empowers us to explore the meaning of "moral community" and "peace education" within the context of the village of Neve Shalom/Wahat Al-Salam. The uniqueness of this school is based on a genuine attempt at partnership between two peoples whose cultures are in geo-political and socio-historic conflict. My intention is to explore the ways in which discussion, moral negotiation and collaborative decision-making formed a basis for creating a spirit of community within the village and in the school. The main goal of this chapter therefore is to explore the ethos of the school as embedded within the larger social organization of the village. I describe the interconnected settings of school and village as a 'moral community' within a larger social-political setting of inter-group conflict. One major focus is on the moral perspectives of the participants in Neve Shalom/Wahat Al-Salam who are involved in a highly innovative discourse of peacemaking through education.

The village and its schools as a "moral" endeavour appear to reflect the need to bring about an understanding of the 'self' in relation to the 'other' in terms of Israeli and Palestinian conflict resolution. It is this quest for understanding between the two cultural/national groups and for awareness of the complexity of the Jewish-Arab issue throughout the Middle East which is at the heart of the peaceful co-existence between the villagers. In allowing my participants to share their multiple voices with me, I struggle to understand the moral dilemmas and complex interrelationships in their lived experiences. As a result of the constant social and political tensions that arise out of the Israeli-Palestinian conflict, moral negotiation in the village continues at all levels of discourse. I am struck by how the villagers are constantly negotiating the space between the tensions of competing national aspirations and their personal attempts at co-existence and good-will. In spite of all the moral complexities and conflicts, my researcher self has become more and more convinced that, at bottom, this is a caring educational community that is dedicated to peaceful co-existence. It may very well be the case that this school has an important role to play in the moral education of culturally diverse communities not only in other parts of Israel but also in the international arena. Indeed, the ongoing quest for peace and justice, evidenced through their personal, social and educational activities, provides the villagers with countless opportunities to interpret and contemplate their cultural and historical destinies. Their stories are simple and complex, ordinary and extraordinary, mundane and heroic, foreign and familiar, full of tension and of hope. I feel honoured to have been among them.

References

Anzaldua, G. (1987). Borderlands/La Frontera: *The New Mestiza. San Francisco*: San Francisco/Aunt Lute.

Bakhtin, M. (1981). *The Dialogic Imagination.* Austin: University of Texas Press.

——(1986). *Speech Genres and Other Late Essays*, trans. V. McGee. Austin: University of Texas Press.

Belenky, M. F., Clinchy, B. McV., Goldberger, N. R., and Tarule, J. M. (1986). *Women's Ways of Knowing: The development of self, voice and mind.* New York: Basic Books.

Benvenisti, M. (1995). *Intimate Enemies: Jews and Arabs in a shared land.* Berkeley: University of California Press.

Britzman, D. (1998). "On Doing Something More," in W. Ayers and J. Miller (Eds.), *Maxine Greene: A light in the dark times.* New York: Teachers College Press, pp. 97–107.

Buber, M. (1958). *I and Thou.* New York: Charles Scribner's Sons.

——(1965). *The Knowledge of Man.* New York: Harper & Row.

Byram, M. S. (1993). "Foreign Language Teaching and Multicultural Education," in A. S. King and J. Reiss (Eds.), *The Multicultural Dimension of the National Curriculum*. London: Falmer Press, pp. 73–86.

Clandinin, D. J. and Connelly, F. M. (1995). "Personal Experience Methods," in N. K. Denzen and Y. S. Lincoln (Eds.), *Handbook of Qualitative Research*. Thousand Oaks, CA: Sage Publications, pp. 413–27.

——(2000). *Narrative Inquiry: Experience and story in qualitative research*. San Francisco: Jossey-Bass.

Coles, R. (1989). *The Call of Stories: Teaching and the moral imagination*. Boston: Houghton Mifflin Co.

——(1998). *Doing Documentary Work*. Oxford: Oxford University Press.

Connelly, F. M. and Clandinin, D. J. (1988). *Teachers as Curriculum Planners: Narratives of experience*. New York: Teachers College Press.

——(1990). "Stories of Experience and Narrative Inquiry." Educational Researcher, 19 (5 June/July), pp. 2–14.

——(1995). *Teachers' Professional Knowledge Landscapes*. New York: Teachers College Press.

Denzin, N. and Lincoln, Y. (1995). *Handbook of Qualitative Research*. Thousand Oaks, CA: Sage.

Dewey, J. (1909/1975). *Moral Principles in Education*. Carbondale: Southern Illinois University Press, Arcturus Books.

——(1938). *Experience and Education*. New York: Collier Books.

Dilthey, W. (1910/1977). "The Understanding of Other Persons and their Expressions of Life," in W. Dilthey, *Descriptive Psychology and Historical Understanding*, trans. R. Zaner and K. Heiges. The Hague: Martinus Nijhoff.

Eisner, E. (1991). *The Enlightened Eye: Qualitative inquiry and the enhancement of educational practice*. New York: Maxwell MacMillan.

Eisner, E. W. and Peshkin, A. (Eds.). (1990). *Qualitative Inquiry in Education: The continuing debate*. New York: Teachers College Press.

Feuerverger, G. (1995). "Oasis of Peace: A Community of Moral Education in Israel," Journal of Moral Education, 24(2), 113–41.

——(1997). "An Educational Program for Peace: Jewish-Arab Conflict Resolution in Israel," Theory into Practice, 36(1), 17–25.

——(2001a). "My Yiddish Voice," in M. Morris and J. Weaver (Eds.), *Difficult Memories: Talk in a (post) Holocaust era*. New York: Peter Lang.

——(2001b). *Oasis of Dreams: Teaching and learning peace in a Jewish-Palestinian village in Israel*. New York: RoutledgeFalmer.

Freire, P. (1970). *Pedagogy of the Oppressed*. New York: Seabury Press.

Freire, P. and Macedo, D. (1987). *Literacy: Reading the word and the world*. South Hadley, MA: Bergin and Garvey.

Geertz, C. (1988). *Works and Lives: The anthropologist as author*. Stanford, CA: Stanford University Press.

——(1995). *After the Fact: Two countries, four decades, one anthropologist*. Cambridge, MA: Harvard University Press.

Gilligan, C. (1982). *In a Different Voice: Psychological theory and women's development*. Cambridge, MA: Harvard University Press.

Giroux, H. A. (1991). "Democracy and the Discourse of Cultural Difference: Towards a Politics of Border Pedagogy," British Journal of Sociology of Education, 12(4), 501–19.

Greene, M. (2000). *Releasing the Imagination: Essays on education, the arts, and social change*. San Francisco: Jossey-Bass.

Gumperz, J. (1977). "Sociocultural Knowledge in Conversational Inference," in M. Saville-Troike (Ed.), *Twenty-Eighth Annual Roundtable Monograph Series in Language and Linguistics*. Washington, DC: Georgetown University Press.

Heath, S. B. (1983). *Ways with Words: Language, life and work in communities and classrooms*. Cambridge: Cambridge University Press.

Huberman, A. M. and Miles, M. B. (1984). *Innovation up Close*. New York: Plenum.

Janesick, V. J. (1991). "Ethnographic Inquiry: Understanding Culture and Experience," in E. Short (Ed.), *Forms of Curriculum Inquiry*. Albany: SUNY Press, pp. 101–19.

Kaiser, S. and Short, K. (1998). "Exploring Culture through Children's Connections," Language Arts, 75(3), 185–92.

Kohlberg, L. (1985). "The Just Community Approach to Moral Education in Theory and Practice," in M. Berkowitz, and F. Oser (Eds.), *Moral Education: Theory and application*. Hillsdale, NJ: Lawrence Erlbaum.

Kozol, J. (1991). *Savage Inequalities: Children in America's schools*. New York: Crown Publishers.

Kridel, C. (Ed.). (1998b). *Writing Educational Biography: Explorations in qualitative research*. New York: Garland.

Kristeva, J. (1991). *Strangers to Ourselves*, trans. Leon S. Roudiez. New York: Columbia University Press.

Lawrence-Lightfoot, S. and Hoffman Davis, J. (2002). *The Art and Science of Portraiture*. San Francisco: Jossey-Bass.

McLaren, P. (1999). Educational Researcher, 28(2), 49–54.

Morrison, T. (1987). *Beloved*. New York: Alfred K. Knopf.

Nieto, S. (1992). *Affirming Diversity: The sociopolitical context of multicultural education*. White Plains, NY: Longman.

Noddings, N. (1991). "Stories in Dialogue: Caring and Interpersonal Reasoning," in C. Witherell and N. Noddings (Eds.), *Stories Lives Tell: Narrative and dialogue in education*. New York: Teachers College Press.

——(2003). *Happiness and Education*. Cambridge: Cambridge University Press.

Palmer, P. (1998). *The Courage to Teach*. San Francisco: Jossey-Bass.

Pinar, W. F. (1988). *Curriculum: Toward new identities*. New York: Garland.

Polkinghorne, D. E. (1988). *Narrative Knowing and the Human Sciences*. Albany: State University of New York Press.

Potok, R. N. (1988). "Borders, Exiles, Minor Literatures: The Case of Palestinian-Israeli Writing," in E. Barkan and M. D. Shelton (Eds.), *Borders, Exiles, Diasporas*. Stanford, CA: Stanford University Press, pp. 291–310.

Richardson, V. (1994). "Conducting Research on Practice," Educational Researcher, 23 (5), 5–10.

Rosaldo, R. (1989/1993). *Culture and Truth: The remaking of social analysis*. London: Routledge.

Sarbin, T. R. (Ed.). (1986). *Narrative Psychology: The storied nature of human conduct*. New York: Praeger.

Schön, D. (Ed.). (1991). *The Reflective Turn: Case studies in and on educational practice*. New York: Teachers College Press.

Shipler, D. K. (1986). *Arab and Jew: Wounded spirits in a promised land*. New York: Times Books.

Tabachnick, B. R. and Zeichner, K. M. (1993). "Preparing Teachers for Cultural Diversity," in P. Gilroy and M. Smith (Eds.), *International Analyses of Teacher Education* (JET Papers One), London: Carfax Publishing, pp. 113–24.

Tappan, M. and Brown, L. (1989). "Stories Told and Lessons Learned: Toward a Narrative Approach to Moral Development and Moral Education," Harvard Educational Review, 59: 182–205.

Van Manen, M. (1990). *Researching Lived Experience: Human science for an action sensitive pedagogy*. London: University of Western Ontario.

Vygotsky, L. S. (1962). *Thought and Language*, trans. A. Kozulin. Cambridge, MA: The MIT Press.

Witherell, C. (1991). "Narrative and the Moral Realm: Tales of Caring and Justice," Journal of Moral Education, 20(3): 237–42.

Witherell, C. and Noddings, N. (Eds.). (1999). *Stories Lives Tell: Narrative and dialogue in education*. New York: Teachers College Press:

Yin, R. K. (1984). *Case Study Research*. London: Sage.

4 Learning Human Rights Praxis

Magnus Haavelsrud

In this chapter, I shall reflect on how education can contribute to the potential of the human being to become a protector and not a violator of human rights. This potential, I believe, is at least to some extent, conditioned by the quality of learning experiences. It is therefore important to consider how the educator comprehends the field of human rights and which assumptions are made about which qualities of the human being are in harmony with human rights practices.

I shall approach the discussion of this topic from three angles. The first discusses the comprehension of human rights in terms of how human rights are understood in relation to the overall concepts of peace and violence including issues of development[1] and disarmament. Human rights, development and disarmament are seen as overlapping as opposed to isolated from each other. And these issues are seen as multi-level including the observable manifestation of problems and conflicts in the specific contextual conditions of the learner—which we shall argue is of utmost importance in educational work. Second, differing—and maybe contradictory—assumptions made about the basic qualities of the human being (the learner) are discussed. And, third, I conclude that learning human rights praxis is in harmony with a holistic comprehension viewing human rights as closely integrated with major issues such as development and disarmament in a multi-level approach requiring analysis of both synchronous and diachronic relations (Haavelsrud, 1975).

The educator, therefore, needs to develop an understanding of human rights in overlapping integration with other issues such as development and disarmament. It also requires that the manifestation of this substance in the specific contextual conditions in which the learner is situated is recognized as valid human rights knowledge. It also requires a dialogical communication form which is based on actual problems and conflicts in that context. Such learning experiences would open spaces for the learners to actively contribute in a praxis which involves transformation towards more human rights practices in the context in which the learner is situated. This kind of educational experience aims to recognize the learner as a subject whose historical role it is to transform the world when problems and challenges are met (Freire, 1972). The professional formation of teachers is therefore an important venue for preparing prospective teachers to meet the difficult practical task of planning and implementing learning experiences in support of socialization of the human being to become a human rights protector and practitioner.

COMPREHENDING HUMAN RIGHTS

How are human rights and their violations understood? In this section I shall discuss this question in light of: (1) the broader concepts of peace and violence; (2) the question of recognition of the other; (3) the question of responsibility; and (4) the dialectic relations between micro and macro.

1. **Concepts of Peace and Violence.** Human rights, development and disarmament are integral and overlapping parts of the wider concept of peace (Haavelsrud, 1996). Furthermore, it is an understanding in the peace research tradition that peace and violence are opposites. Galtung (1996) points to three major forms of violence, viz. direct, structural and cultural. Similar to the interdependence of human rights with development and disarmament, there is a link between direct, structural and cultural violence. To understand the causes of any form of violence requires an investigation into the relationship between the three forms. This means that if we set out to understand the causes of direct violence, we must ensure that the previous, present and planned cultural and structural violence is seen as relevant in the investigation of the causes. If we are to understand the causes of structural violence, we must be open to the idea that its causes are related to the use of past, present and planned direct and cultural violence. If we want to know the causes of cultural violence, we cannot exclude investigations into the impact of past, present and planned direct and structural violence.

    It is not unusual to hear politicians talk of direct violence as an isolated case without connections to structural and cultural violence. An easy solution is to declare an act of direct violence as "evil" without searching for possible causes and/or motives of this "evil" and isolate the act as a product of the quality of specific individuals and groups—even states (e.g. the idea of an axis of evil). This strong classification (Bernstein, 1996; Haavelsrud, 2001) between direct violence and other forms of violence oftentimes carries the power of a hegemonic position which may be used to influence cultural agencies such as the media and schools in such a way that the strength of the communication control shapes the consciousness of the receiver according to the strong classification made in the first place. According to Basil Bernstein, we can say that the classification carries the power and the communication control secures the transmission of this power. This most important symbolic battle for the mind may temporarily divert seeds of resistance and implant the simplification necessary for the continuation of the classifier's hegemony. For some time it may be difficult to question the classifications of a hegemonic—sometimes totalitarian—ruler. Historical experience, however, seems to support the idea that, at least in the long run, the dominance of simplifications produces seeds of resistance and alternatives beyond the control of the ruler (examples, apartheid in South Africa, dictatorships or other totalitarian regimes that too many have experienced in recent decades).

As there are three forms of violence, we may also talk of three forms of "peace," i.e. the peace of the absence of direct violence (no bombs and no fists), the peace of the presence of social justice (equality of material needs and solidarity), and the peace of cultural respect (diversity, cultural autonomy and participation). An occupier may say that the occupation will end only if direct violence from the occupied is ended. Groups among the occupied may say that direct violence will end when the direct, structural and cultural violence of the occupier has ended. The occupier and the occupied have differing conceptions of peace without recognizing, respecting or maybe even understanding the other's opinion and feelings.

2. **The Question of Recognition.** In the peace education tradition, all human beings are seen to be in need of peace education. If some human beings were to express an image of self—indicating superiority over other human beings, this image would in itself be an important problem to deal with (Haavelsrud, 1996). The concept of "the civilized world" or "the first world" indicates superiority over those parts that are not civilized. Positive descriptions of one's own ethnic group, social class, gender, and sexual preference may be combined with explicit negative descriptions of another ethnic group, social class, gender, and sexual preference. Or the explicit positive description of self implies an implicit negative attitude towards others. Such a positive image of self combined with explicit or implicit negative images of others indicates superiority, especially when it comes from a hegemonic ruler who even may be an occupier.

Direct violence in any conflict is evidence of non-recognition of the other. This lack of recognition is also evidenced in everyday cultural expressions of a life as a "comfortable experience," for instance, illustrated descriptions of the micro reality of Israeli settlements in the West Bank:

> The biblical landscape is charming. From the window you can gaze through the geraniums and bougainvillea and not see the occupation. Travelling on the fast highway that takes you from Ramot on Jerusalem's northern edge to Gilo on the southern edge, a 12-minute trip just west of the Palestinian roadblocks, it's hard to comprehend the humiliating experience of the despised Arab who must creep for hours along the pocked, blockaded roads assigned to him. One road for the occupier, one road for the occupied ... Israel, having ceased to care about the children of the Palestinians, should not be surprised when they come washed in hatred and blow themselves up in the centers of Israeli escapism ... We could kill a thousand ringleaders and engineers

a day and nothing will be solved, because the leaders come up from below—from the wells of hatred and anger, from the "infrastructures" of injustice and moral corruption.

(Burg, 2003)

This glimpse of an everyday moment in occupied land illustrates how the macro manifests itself in the micro and how the micro actors choose to ignore the occupation of the land of others. This psychological mechanism may be more understandable than the militaristic policies designed to maintain this status quo of occupation including poverty, injustice and cultural hegemony. These policies contribute to the maintenance of "a thunderously failed reality" which means that they contribute to worsen the problem rather than solving it (ibid.). As the author of the above quote was a well-known politician among the occupiers and a former Speaker of the Knesset, his observations of human rights violations as manifested in the everyday experience of the occupied demonstrates a recognition both of failed policies and of the opinion and feelings of the occupied (see also Burg, 2008). This is an example of an attempt to integrate the analysis of human rights violations at the policy level (macro) with the level of everyday micro realities (micro). This is one important quality of the kind of human rights learning that we discuss in this chapter on learning human rights praxis.

3. **Responsibility.** Globally, the death of more than 30,000 children every day under the age of 5 from preventable causes is an example of structural violence involving policy priorities in development, disarmament and human rights. It would be difficult to argue that the root cause of the misery of the world is the lack of resources to the military. A global structure characterized by enormous military spending in the midst of unbelievable misery does not leave any part of that structure without responsibility—certainly not the most dominant powers in that structure. The greatest contributors and supporters of an order characterized by so much misery need to accept a fair amount of responsibility for maintaining or changing it. This line of thought directs our attention to the human rights violations inherent at the policy level resulting in the direct, structural and cultural violence causing human misery. We know very well who these actors are as they figure daily on the front pages of most quality newspapers around the world. And they receive prime time television attention. These actors need as much attention—if not more attention—in human rights education as they receive in the quality press. The reason is that they are all involved in contributing towards global policies that have a huge impact on either human rights violations or in human rights protection. Some of them contribute to policy-making leading to violations which of course need attention in human rights education. It becomes a great task in human rights education to distinguish between policy initiatives that violate or protect human rights at various levels of governance—from the transnational to the municipal levels.

4. Micro–macro relations. Peace and violence are expressed through the actions, emotions and thoughts of human beings of all ages. The human being is, so to speak, at the epicenter of peace and violence. This means that micro reality is the focus in studies of peace and violence. The carrier of both peace and violence is always a human being. A human being is an actor in the micro even though a specific micro may be in a palace or government house as opposed to in a kitchen of a poor family without food for hungry children. Some human beings are located in macro positions and carry out macro duties and responsibilities. But this does not mean that they are not also actors in the micro: No macro interactions can exist in isolation from micro interactions among the human beings populating that macro space. A macro would not exist without a micro manifestation—beautifully described in The Emperor referring to interactions between the people populating the castle before the downfall of Haile Selassie (Kapuscinski, 1989). The Emperor or King relates to other human beings in his daily work, just as the Pope or a prime minister of a nation—and the people relating to such top figures also interact with each other.

It may be argued that some micro realities are more important than others because the actions, thoughts, emotions and will of the actors may be controlled by strong forces beyond the will of the individual actor.[2] In addition, the consequences of actions taken in some micro realities may be of greater importance than actions taken in other micro realities because the action will affect more people or deal with more serious issues than other micro realities. Some other micro realities may seem less important because the actions, thoughts, emotions and will of the actors may seem to have consequences for a smaller number of people and the issues dealt with may appear less important.

Even if this were true in most cases, there are exceptions that prove the opposite, viz. that the macro in the micro may be more important than the micro in the macro. This means that when resistance to human rights violations takes refuge in prisons, mountains, forests and cities or simply in the homes and among friends, these micro realities have the potential to sow seeds for future developments beyond the control of those macro figures. Humanity had to fight such dictators as Pinochet, Videla, Hitler and Pol Pot. Mandela's imprisonment in a small cell lasted for 27 years. This magnificent prisoner in the small cell turned into a macro actor in the end, even before his status as prisoner had ended as he decided to negotiate with De Klerk even though he had no green light from the African National Congress (Mandela, 1995).

ASSUMPTIONS ABOUT THE HUMAN BEING

Few, if any, psychologists and social scientists would disagree with the statement that the formation of the basic psychological framework of the human being happens in the close relationships that the child experiences in the first years of life. This mental schema will be the basis upon which the human being develops towards an adult. As the quality of human interactions vary a great deal from one micro reality to another, it is to be assumed that the quality of the frames created would also vary. In any case, informal education in the family should be recognized as an important source shaping the frame of the human being in support of becoming a protector or violator of human rights. When the teacher meets the children in Grade 1 (or in kindergarten), s/he will have to work with that psychological frame which has already been created in the home. And the homes differ in their socialization practices, also in their assumptions about the basic qualities of a human being.

This variation in socialization practices in the homes reflects differing views in social science. Many books have been published on models of humanity (Chapman and Jones, 1980; Dagenais, 1972; Hollis, 1977; Nash, 1968; Skidmore, 1975). Much of the literature is, however, rooted in Western cosmology. Views range from one extreme to another. Some would argue that the human being is a free agent with a free will and can act according to a self that cannot be understood by scientific means, whereas others would see the human being "operating within a wholly determined, orderly universe. All human behaviour is externally caused and controlled ... One of Skinner's strongest points is the claim that it is not a question of freedom or control, but of who is to control us" (Nash, 1968: 407).

This is only one example of fundamental different assumptions made about the human being. Philosophers, social scientists and psychologists have developed a variety of conceptions of what the basic qualities of the human being are. The human rights teacher is in a practical position requiring some clarification as to which assumptions about the human being should be made. In order to illustrate how difficult it is to arrive at a clarification about this basic issue, I shall compare the assumptions made about the quality of the human being in the work of two great social scientists—Durkheim and Mead.[3] I have selected these two because they belong to different social science paradigms. Durkheim argued explicitly for specific pedagogic preferences whereas only after his death has Mead's theory become an important inspiration in pedagogical discourse, as, for instance, in the New Sociology of Education which developed at the beginning of the 1970s. The comparison between the two theories illustrates the difficult challenge to the teacher: Which assumptions are selected about the essential qualities of the learner when designing learning activities?

Durkheim sees the human being as limitless and greedy. The human being needs to learn self-constraint in order to fit into the common good and the community. The concept of organic solidarity contains the moral norms of modern society. The moral principles involved in organic solidarity are based on social norms that give all human beings responsibilities. The norms are social facts—not only abstractions. The norms function to regulate and standardize the actions of the citizens. Moral behaviors are collective habits.

These habits must be learned through regularity and authority that together constitute discipline. Discipline will function to limit the limitless human being. In this way, discipline is seen as a condition for happiness and moral health. Discipline must be learned in school and in this way Durkheim is an authoritarian educator. Durkheim recognized different moral collectives: the family, the political party, the nation, and humanity. He concentrated mainly on the nation and the primary school's obligation to teach organic solidarity and the norms of society to all students in order to further the collective interest and avoid the disintegration of society.

In spite of the fact that he argues for an authoritarian pedagogy, Durkheim is a believer in the free will of the person to act within acceptable norms. He sees moral acts as free acts in that they are based in the will of the consciousness. But it seems that this consciousness is conditioned by a specific type of Durkheimean education characterized by the understanding of the collective interest of society and the habitual behaviors in the practice of social norms developed in a rather authoritarian pedagogy. So the free will would be free within these limits. The formation of unruly children to follow moral behavior is achieved through the authority of the adult parent, relative or teacher through model behavior and through force, regularity, authority, and discipline.

France had decided to introduce confession-free schools and Durkheim found himself in a context in need of norms to replace the norms previously derived from religion. It is interesting to ponder how social scientists have been influenced by the context in which they live. It may be that the paradigmatic gap between Durkheim and Mead could be partly explained by the influence of such contextual differences. The cultural continuity of France may be seen as the opposite of the multicultural discontinuities of Chicago. One of the challenges in Mead's context was a Chicago that had doubled its population from 500,000 to 1 million in 10 years (1880–90). Immigrants from a large number of cultures met each other in the big slaughterhouses and in the city, prepared to realize the American dream. They spoke different languages, had different habits and lifestyles. Mead developed the idea of the human being as a creator of the future as well as the creator of himself or herself. In this creation the human being develops an identity—a self–based on his or her interactions with others. By taking the perspective of the other, it becomes to some extent a guide in understanding and action. The human being considers the other before acting. Mead says that the human being is social and begins developing this aspect as a small baby, making gestures and sounds to others, especially the parents. Through interpreting the other, the person constitutes his or her own identity—the self. In the end, the human being will understand and act according to how he or she has developed an understanding of the other and how s/he has acquired "the attitude of the whole community." Mead's human being is much more a subject in the interactive process than Durkheim's human being who becomes an object of norms external to the human being.

Mead sees the human being as a social person who in communication with others constructs and shapes society. The self begins developing in the first few months of life through the gestures that babies address to others, especially the mother. As the baby receives responses to the gestures, the baby learns that the other has a pattern in their responses. Soon the baby develops expectations of the other—expectations that later develop into play in which the role of known persons can be acted out, such as mother, father, and child. Even later, the interactions with others are tried in games in which the rules create a more formal base for developing expectations of the others in the game.

Such interactive experiences of a human being—in play, in games, in all moments of life—are decisive for the constitution of the self of that human being. The interactions inform the person of what is expected by the others and these expectations would to some extent determine one's own actions and how my own self would fit into the expectations of the others. The development of the self is therefore a product of the interactions with others in which "the perspective of the other" is taken, resulting in acquiring "the attitude of the whole community." The human being is here seen as a contributor to the construction of oneself in interaction with others. But this human being as subject is always limited to this interaction with others and it is still a mystery how Mead can break out of the vicious circle of oppressive relationships.

Although both Durkheim and Mead are firmly rooted in a Western cosmology that has shown little interest in other cosmologies around the world, they are very different in their view of how the human being develops to become a human being. Mead inspired the social definition paradigm whereas Durkheim is a founder of functionalism. Durkheim sees the human being as an object of the moral norms of society. These norms are external to the human being and they are transferred by force, discipline, and authority to the pupil. As a functionalist, Durkheim focuses on how the whole and the parts interrelate. But he does not include nature as part of the whole. And he has not much to say about humanity as a whole: His analysis does not include the relation between humanity as a whole and specific societies. He is mainly concerned about his "fatherland": France.

So the discussion of the basic qualities of the human being has excluded the relations between the human being and nature. In the above comparison between Durkheim and Mead, nature is absent. In the present context, it would seem irresponsible to exclude nature from this discussion of the basic qualities of the human being. It is not only irresponsible, but impossible in terms of oriental philosophy where the human being and his/her environment are conceptualized as an integrated whole:

> While we may perceive our mind, body and environment to have separate existences, the view of nature that we have adopted holds that a human being does not exist apart and aloof from the natural world but is part

of it. From this it follows that our mind and body together with the surrounding environment are integral to each other and identified as one.

(Nomura, 2002: 49)

Nomura's concept of the "environment" is divided into the human, the material, and the natural. The integration of the inner world of the individual and the outer world of the environment corresponds to the integration of subjectivity and objectivity. The simultaneous interdependence and the inseparability of subject and object are ensured through the senses of the human being (see, hear, smell, taste, touch). This concept of seeing "humans in oneness with nature is based on the principle of identified relationship that the two are one, that their relations are mutually and indivisibly correlated" (Nomura, 1998: 125).

Neither Durkheim nor Mead view socialization explicitly in relation to the question of peace and violence. Nomura, however, makes an explicit connection between socialization and the question of peace and violence. Peace is defined as a "balanced state between mind, body and environment" (ibid.: 129). This definition suggests that there is a principle of co-existence underlying peace. Violence against one of the parts would be violence against the whole, including the self, as, for instance: "Our ignorant and reckless exploitation is destroying the environment on which we depend, threatening our own survival as well as that of all living things" (ibid.: 127).

The principle of co-existence for all humankind is seen as a potential and "valuable principle for peace" (ibid.: 131) depending upon the success of life-long integrated education. Without such education, humans are going to continue to break wholes into parts and deal with isolated and segregated cases rather than interdependencies and wholes. The ignorance resulting from fragmentation and separateness is therefore a basic cause of violence. The wisdom of integration and co-existence achieved through education could become a basic cause of peace. Because of the prominence of the human being both as a creator and protector of peace as well as violence, it is important to include differing perspectives on how a human being is seen and which qualities he or she has. Each perspective has implicitly or explicitly directions for how to educate and form the human being.

CONCLUSION

It has been argued that human rights need to be understood in relation to other peace issues such as disarmament and development and in relation to specific contexts. It has also been argued that human rights education—like all education—needs to clarify its conception of the basic qualities of the human being.

How can teachers in the formal educational system be prepared to take on the difficult task of designing learning experiences that will support socialization of children and youth to become human rights protectors? Based on the above, our answer would be two-fold: (1) providing a teacher education that would include in its curriculum questions of comprehending human rights as an integral part of the concept of peace, which also includes development and disarmament issues on all levels, ranging from the local to the global; and (2) making space in the teacher education curriculum for the teacher to develop his or her understanding of the basic qualities of the human being and how qualities for the socialization of the human being as a human rights protector can be cultivated in planning and implementing educational experiences in school.

Learning experiences in teacher education to achieve these two goals—one related to the content of human rights and the other related to the form in which this content is communicated—could depart from the following "old" insight:

> It is most uncertain whether the educational invention made by those who emphasize teaching or the educational invention made by those who emphasize learning will survive. But the more rapidly we can erase from our society those discrepancies in position and privilege which tend to perpetuate and strengthen the power and manipulative aspects of education, the more hope we may have that that other invention—the use of education for unknown ends which shall exalt man above his present stature—may survive.
>
> (Mead, 1943)

In our continued attempts to follow up on Margaret Mead's challenge, we are faced with the most basic questions that social science has to offer. One basic question is to what extent the assumption will be made that the individual is a rational or even a strategic actor as opposed to the emotional and expressive kind—a human being who might even be non-rational. Another basic question is to what extent objective and material structures cause human behavior in a deterministic fashion or whether individual behavior is more an expression of a symbolic meaning structure which could be constructed in interaction with others. Guneriussen (1996: 299–305) poses such questions toward the end of his book on the basic problems in social science without providing 'correct' answers. So far, we do not know how social reality is constructed. Some would assume that objective laws can be found for how this reality comes about—almost analogous to a physical-mechanical system. Others would see social reality as a text which is constantly being interpreted by individuals in interaction. The division in the basic approach to understanding social reality is closely associated with the question of whether, or to what extent, the individual actor is a product of his or her surroundings or whether, or to what extent, the individual is a subject and a creator of this reality.

These limits to the scientific understanding of man (Stent, 1975: 1052–57) are the shaky ground on which the educator should base his/her work in sorting valid educational principles from invalid ones in order to implement a program of action that in itself will become a factor, maybe an essential factor, in the dynamics of individual and collective life. It seems as though the safest pedagogic approach would be to admit that so far we do not know enough about the human being to be able to assume either that s/he is a strategic and rational individual or an emotional actor that would place a high value on communitarian ideals. The human being could be both at the same time, allowing a dialectic process to take place in which both could be true. Another alternative could be that s/he could be more strategic in certain contexts and more expressive in others. It could be possible that material structures form the human being at the same time as symbolic meaning structures are created as well as reproduced. Pedagogical thought would then also have to be multi-paradigmatic by admitting that there could be some truth to alternative answers to even basic questions. This pedagogic approach would be inclusive in the sense that it would allow a dialogue also about the constitution of the human species. Considering the status of our knowledge of the human being, it seems logical to conclude that both the education of teachers and the education in the formal school system need to secure the development of knowledge in a dialogical format—this in order to secure an open and multi-paradigmatic approach to such questions.

Such a multi-paradigmatic approach would recognize that the oriental perspective of integration is a more complete integrative perspective than the peace research focus on seeing human rights as an integral part of the wider concept of peace including development and disarmament issues. In terms of comprehending the issue of human rights in its relevance to the broader concept of peace, the oriental perspective is closer to the peace education tradition which has developed in close relation to the great contribution of Paulo Freire. The impatience of Freire in terms of action and transformation not only of self but of the world, makes his contribution a guiding light compared with the Western perspectives of Durkheim and Mead discussed above. Freire says that it is the vocation of the human being to be an historical subject. This means that the human being is part of a praxis which results in the transformation of both the individual subject and the world in which the human being reflects and acts. Durkheim and Mead do not come close to this basic pedagogical task of conscientization. But the Durkheimian understanding of organic solidarity and the importance of the perspective of the other in Mead add to our understanding even though their perspective as a whole may be alien to modern pedagogy as developed in the Freirean concept of dialogue (reflection and action), i.e. praxis. It is basic to dialogic pedagogy to see the human being as a subject whose main purpose and quality it is to contribute to the transformation of the world rather than adapting to its deficiencies. Paulo Freire views the human being as an historical subject whose ontological vocation it is to help transform the world. The human being as creator of the future presupposes that the culture of silence is broken through a dialogical method of liberation together with others in the same context. The dialogue is itself a creation that will have an impact on the world of the future. The creation of the world and the status as a subject are realized through dialogue as praxis involving both reflection and action upon contradictions in society.

This may be the most important lesson for teacher education. Democracy can be strengthened through a solid profession of teachers whose professionalism is strong enough to resist attempts—to the degree possible depending upon contextual conditions—to use the educational system to transmit the power of oppressive forces. In this way, the teaching profession may become the key to the creation of a foundation of democracy that can survive even the strongest political turbulence inherent in democratic processes. But this would imply that teacher education itself needs to practice principles of critical dialogue. This pedagogy would protect and support the power of the human being to dream and to think, recognizing that people dream about a different world than the one we have now—and they always have done. People always had dreams and some of them became more than dreams—they became reality. When a dream becomes reality, the power of human consciousness has been at work. Without the power to dream and think about the world as it ought to be, the present would not change.

But the dreams or visions of the future are not independent of present realities, but based in these realities. As we look around us, we see many things that are wrong and could be better. The human ability to observe these facts in our workplace, in our home, in our school, in our neighborhood, in our community, in our own country and in other countries and between countries and in the world makes all of us a witness to many things. Sometimes we become more than a witness—willingly or not. We become a participant in interactions with others. This interaction may change present reality and also future reality as reflection and action combine in transforming dreams into concrete changes modifying the now and the future as well. Witnessing and participating give us an expertise learned from our experience as witnesses and participants in the world. This accumulated experience is one background for changing the immediate reality of today as well as the more distant reality of the future.

In educational work we have a special responsibility to ensure that the educational system is free of cultural violence. Unfortunately, we know too well that there are many examples of educational systems that have functioned to support human rights violations either by ignoring these violations or by actively practicing discrimination of the cultural identities of specific groups of people. And it is a challenge to all formal educational systems to strive towards ideals of equal educational opportunity and fairness in its relations with the differences between cultural preferences of various categories of people in society. Any education, whether informal, non-formal or formal, can either support or overlook the human rights agenda as this agenda relates to the lives of pupils, students, parents, teachers and citizens. Educational practices in support of human rights will emphasize critical thought about the present and dreams for a different future in developing a greater capacity for participating in the creation of more democracy—at all levels. This education opens dialogue and reflection about what is wrong, ugly and false as opposed to what is right, beautiful and true, recognizing the expertise of experiencing everyday life. The success of this critical thinking depends upon the resilience of the frame of the human being to power and control that attempt to use cultural agencies to legitimate both direct and structural violence. Education is the most important cultural agency and it may not go too far to state that the counter-power from education may be the last hope of humanity in a world that seems to be dominated by hegemonic simplifications about violence and peace without support in what we know about this topic today.

Notes

1 The concept of development is not restricted to the old-fashioned concept of economic development, but includes development in the broad and holistic sense including ecological, social, cultural, political and economic development (see e.g. Part III in Galtung (1996) and Chapter 14 in Haavelsrud (1996)).
2 In a play by Brecht on the life of Galileo Galilei, the court of the Inquisition assembles in order to make a decision on what to do with the scientist. The Pope is part of the court and at the beginning—actually before he has put on his official garments—he defends Galilei. As the Pope gets ready for the meeting and appears in full Pope clothing, his liberal attitude disappears. When he finally wears full ornate, he orders that Galilei should be shown the instruments of torture. This story shows the tension between the Pope as person with individual freedom of action and the Pope as the actor who is expected by the church community to act as required. In one instance, the Pope is the individual, in the other closely tied to a structure and therefore losing his individuality (Bjørndal, 1997: 11; 2003).
3 In the following discussion of Durkheim's view of the human being, I have made good use of Durkheim (1979) and Løvlie (1989). Mead (1943) and Vaage (1996) have been of good use in the following interpretation of Mead's view of the human being.

References

Bernstein, Basil (1996). *Pedagogy, Symbolic Control and Identity: Theory, research, critique*. London: Taylor & Francis.

Bjørndal, Cato (1997). *Nærhet og distanse til elevroller*. Hovedoppgave: Universitetet i Tromsø.

——(2003). *Regi på klasserommets scene*. Oslo: Unipub forla.

Burg, Avraham (2003). "The End of Zionism: A Failed Israeli Society Is Collapsing," International Herald Tribune, September 6–7.

——(2008). *The Holocaust Is Over, We Must Rise from Its Ashes*. Basingstoke: Macmillan.

Chapman, Antony J., and Jones, Dylan M. (1980). *Models of Man*. London: The British Psychological Society.

Dagenais, James. J. (1972). *Models of Man: A phenomenological critique of some paradigms in the human sciences*. The Hague: Martinus Nijhoff.

Durkheim, Emile (1979). *Essays on Morals and Education*. London: Routledge & Kegan Paul.

Freire, Paulo (1972). *Pedagogy of the Oppressed*. Harmondsworth: Penguin.

Galtung, Johan (1996). *Peace by Peaceful Means*. London: Sage.

Guneriussen, Willy (1996). *Aktør, Handling, Struktur: Grunnlagsproblemer i samfunnsvitenskapene*. Oslo: Tano.

Haavelsrud. Magnus (1975). "Principles of Peace Education," in M. Haavelsrud (Ed.), *Education for Peace: Reflection and action*. London: IPC Science and Technology Press.

——(1996). *Education in Developments*. London: Arena.

——(2001). "Classification Strength and Power Relations," in Ana Morais et al. (Eds.), *Towards a Sociology of Pedagogy: The contribution of Basil Bernstein to research*. New York: Peter Lang, pp. 319—38.

Hollis, Martin (1977). *Models of Man: Philosophical thoughts on social action*. Cambridge: Cambridge University Press.

Kapuscinski, Ryszard (1989). *The Emperor: Downfall of an autocrat*. London: Penguin.

Løvlie, Lars (1989). "Oppdragelse til samhold," in Harald Thuen and Sveinung Vaage (Eds.), *Oppdragelse til det moderne*. Oslo: University Press.

Mandela, Nelson (1995). *Long Walk to Freedom*. London: Abacus.

Mead, Margaret (1943). "Our Educational Emphasis in Primitive Perspective," The American Journal of Sociology, XLVIII(6), 633–39.

Nash, Paul (1968). *Models of Man: Explorations in the Western educational tradition*. New York: John Wiley & Sons, Inc.

Nomura, Yoshiko (1998). *Lifelong Integrated Education as a Creator of the Future: The principles of Nomura lifelong integrated education* 1. London: Trentham Books.

——(2002). *Lifelong Integrated Education as a Creator of the Future: The principles of Nomura lifelong integrated education* II. London: Trentham Books.

Skidmore, William L. (1975). *Sociology's Models of Man*. New York: Gordon and Breach.

Stent, Gunther S. (1975). "The Limits to the Scientific Understanding of Man," Science, 21 March: 1052–57.

Vaage, Sveinung (1989). "G. H. Mead om utdanning og sosialisering," in Harald Thuen and Sveinung Vaage (Eds.), *Oppdragelse til det moderne*. Oslo: University Press.

5   On Human Rights, Philosophy, and Education

The Ethics of Difference after Deconstruction

Peter Pericles Trifonas

This chapter engages the ethical ground of difference for peace, the right to philosophy, and the future of education. It asks, after Jacques Derrida, whether or not it is possible to expose or create a location that still occupies the colonized space of an archive of knowledge and is at the same time alterior to it. If so, how and where (Derrida, 1996)?[1] The syncretic nature of a mondialized subjectivity is the product of a cosmopolitical point of view. Alterity marks a radicalization of difference but with a debt and duty to the historicity of what has gone before. My reading of the ethics of deconstruction and its incursion into the logic of the cosmopolitical will broach the question of human rights, peace, and education to rethink the certainty of "where ought it [to] take place" ("Of the Humanities and the Philosophical Discipline," Derrida, 1996: 1). The ethical problem of who can, should be, or is capable of determining the propriety of the formal location of inquiry is a flash point of controversy and conflict. Deconstruction is always already implicated in the perennial question of democracy and discipline, of peace and pedagogy and, for Derrida, the future of education is articulated as the right to philosophy, thought, and thinking in relation to the difference of the other.

The ground of knowledge engages the logic of alterity. Affirming certainty of understanding safeguards the possibility peaceable speech with an other. Educational institutions and by extension those who teach, work, and live in and, perhaps, for them, as the teaching body (le corps enseignant) bear such a responsibility.[2] The problem of human rights, of institutions, of philosophy entails issues of propriety and domination, therefore of law, ethics, and ultimately, of social justice. The problem of democracy and democraticity relates to the oppositions between culture and knowledge and the disjunctive formativity of a system of public education on an international scale. It is a matter of locating the axiomatic difference of these terms and their inter-relatability within a hospitable space and place that only deconstruction can entreat them to for a productive recognition of alterity. Derrida redefines the heterogeneous scope of this impossible territory wherein the struggle over difference and human rights occurs in the aftermath of Kant's cosmopolitical condition: a hypothetical situation of geo-global interconnectivity or "mondialization" having an "inter-national or inter-state dimension" (Derrida, 1996: 2).

The cosmopolitical is a vision of the world that operationalizes the emanation and diaspora of the polis and politeia as a way of life. The Kantian ideal of the cosmopolitical solidifies the problem of a universal history or "the link among the cities, the poleis of the world, as nations, as people, or as States" (ibid.: 2). A panoptic vision harbors an omniscient hope. One that confirms the epistemologico-historical foundations of an "abstract universalism" (ibid.: 2). The Kantian cosmopolitical forges a template upon which any and all institutions to come can be inscribed forever in principle and action. The future of thinking, however, has to work toward illuminating and transforming rather than dismissing or deriding the historicity of "philosophical acts and archives" (ibid.: 2). Peace is the productive recognition of alterity put into practice. Deconstruction, in questioning the ground of institutions and the reason of their institutionality with respect to the formation of subjectivity, engages the real-world effects produced by the performative force of epistemological discourses and their responsibility as instances of founding and therefore of foundation. The problem of how to reconcile human rights and difference with the Kantian conception of a cosmopolitical point of view demands a positive rather than a negative resolution for peace. The notion of alterity is contrary to the ideal of a natural universalism of thought and action uniting thinking and subjectivity in the image of the global citizen and international institutions. Derrida explains, the Idea (in View) of a Universal History from a Cosmopolitical Point of View [Idee zu einer allgemeinen Geschichte in weltbürgerlicher Absicht] is one of an

> [An] ensemble of Kant's writings that can be described as announcing, that is to say, predicting, prefiguring and prescribing a number of international institutions which only came into being in this century, for the most part after the Second World War. These institutions are already philosophemes, as is the idea of international law or rights that they attempt to put into operation.
>
> (ibid.: 2)

The reference is applicable to the unique case of UNESCO. An institution of the postwar era, it imbibes in its constitutional commitments and formal configurations "an assignable philosophical history" (ibid.: 2) that "impl[ies] sharing a culture and a philosophical language" (ibid.: 2).

DECONSTRUCTING UNESCO

UNESCO facilitates the exchange of a tradition of knowledge and knowing as articulated by a universal archive, mediates for the terms of its reading as production and reproduction, and actualized the cultural domains of its power as global narrative. The scope of this institution involves the working-out of the two types of relation: the question of privilege (who has the right to knowledge?) and the power of location (how? and why?). The pedagogical onus of UNESCO fixes the parameters of an institutional ethic of response and responsibility. The danger is when education is construed as an affable (simple, crude, vulgar) modality of a globalizing cultural production and reproduction without the complexity of resistance or complications of thought. A reduction of the frame of reference to categorical imperatives ignores the limitations and boundaries of a project like UNESCO. When the difference of the cosmopolitical is not taken into account, the idea of universalism does not recognize the alterity of otherness for an essential sameness. UNESCO is a globalistic gathering of multiplicity through the image of a charter (a constitution, treaty, or settlement, a founding document, statement of rights and obligations, laws, etc.). The inter-national act of institution enacts the covenant of relation that is intended to bridge difference and otherness by involving a contractual obligation between philosophy and action that articulates the ethical terms of its responsibility:

All the States that adhere to the charters of these international institutions [such as UNESCO, the United Nations also], commit themselves, in principle and philosophically, to recognize and put into practice in an effective way something like philosophy and a certain philosophy of rights and law, the rights of [wo]man, universal history, etc. The signature of these charters is a philosophical act which makes a commitment to philosophy in a philosophical way. From that moment on, whether they say so or not, know it or not, or conduct themselves consequently or not, these States and these peoples contract a philosophical commitment by dint of joining these charters or participating in these institutions. Therefore, these States contract at the very least a commitment to provide the philosophical culture or education that is required for understanding and putting into operation these commitments made to the international institutions, which are, I repeat, philosophical in essence.

("Of the Humanities and the Philosophical Discipline," Derrida, 1996: 2)

UNESCO is an organization of many parts and partners, nations, states, and peoples whose materiality comprises and cannot but exceed the conceptual and material totality of its essence. It bears the obligation to unite response with responsibility within the milieu of the international and interdisciplinary. This tract will lead to the impossibility of the future possibility of UNESCO and the global diaspora of subjectivity. That is, the institutional interconnections of a democracy-to-come, with a pedagogy-to-come, and the potentially diverging paths of its filiations. The very existence of UNESCO begs for inquiry after the Kantian cosmopolitical point of view. That is, a "plan of nature that aims at the total, perfect political unification of the human species [*die vollkommene bürgerliche Vereinigung in der Menschengattung*]"[3] by conceiving of history as the material unfolding of the transcendental unity of the Idea. Kant's ethical universalism turned toward the question of human rights and difference mobilizes the cosmopolitical. Not only for reconceptualizing the "eternal becoming"[4] of being-in-the-world, but as a new approach to realizing the impossible futures of a "progressive institutionality" to come and the unforeseeability of its educational methods and apparatus.

This does not simply mean a securing of the opportunity for freedom in thinking and teaching. Neither does it defer pedagogically, nor ethically, to the teaching of thinking without reference to the tradition of a Western episteme. Derrida cites the Kantian notion of the cosmopolitical to reawaken and to resituate the Eurocentrism of the concept and its implications for reinscribing the "horizon of a new community" ("Des humanités," Derrida, 1996: 3) of the question—and the impossibility of the question that teaches the Other to question the sources of the Self and the Other. This may sound strange to those who envision and portray deconstruction as a destruction of Western metaphysics, its institutions and its teachings. UNESCO is an institution that is a priori "Kantian in spirit" (ibid.: 3). Which is to say, it predicts a Western trajectory of thinking along a "teleological axis" (ibid.: 3) with respect to the epistemologico-cultural ideal of the "infinite progress" of Being and the temporal procession of beings toward an ideal of perfectability achievable through education. As Derrida explains:

> Whoever would have doubts about such a unification and, above all, about a plan of nature, would have no reason to subscribe even to the fact of sharing a philosophical problematic, of a supposedly universal or universalizable problematic of philosophy. For anybody having doubts about this plan of nature, the whole project of writing a universal—and therefore philosophical—history, and thus as well the project of creating institutions governed by an international—and therefore philosophical—law, would be nothing but a novel.
>
> ("Of the Humanities and the Philosophical Discipline,"
> Derrida, 1996: 2)

An institution is founded on memory and the material conditions of its working-out as a dynamic tradition of theory and practice, philosophy and action. Deconstruction is predicated on taking memory into account: accounting for the causality of its effects, its bias, its exclusions, rendering an account of what makes memory, disrupts it, constructs its limits, openings, how and why it favors.

UNESCO as an international institution is founded on the principles of European philosophy. Its charter and its concepts "are philosophical through and through" ("Des humanités," ibid.: 2), which does not make them universal in scope or essence, despite the reality that UNESCO does attempt to influence, "for the better," the educational landscape of the world. This latter point is important in reading the dimensions of the first. That the aim of this organization is, in theory, altruistic cannot be denied, as the logic of its existence is predicated, in principle, on the presupposition of the idea of an infinite perfectability of human being. It mobilizes a thoroughly Western conceit and philosophical project directed toward the pragmatic rectification of Being as presence and the sending of itself forward in time toward the infinity of progressive becoming.

For Derrida, it is not a matter of questioning the existence of UNESCO outside of the scope of its mission statement and the theoretical grounds of the practical action laid out by the logic of its charter. In ethical, philosophical, and real-world terms, we can easily justify the necessity of its "being-there" on an international, global scale. Especially when considering that its charter upholds the point of view of a cosmopolitical model of membership, governance, and responsibility. Sanctioning, above all, the development and sustenance of democratic means and conditions for securing public access to education globally. It would not make sense to dismiss or defame UNESCO either as an instrument of Western influence and cogitation or as an indicator of the extent of Western domination across the hemispheres with respect to propagating a "certain philosophy of rights and law, the rights of man [Derrida's word], universal history" ("Of the Humanities and the Philosophical Discipline," Derrida, 1996: 2), and so on. A critique—coming down on one side or the other—of its efficacy is not at all useful, but a misleading endeavor seeking an ethical refuge in the evaluative power of a binary form of metaphysical reasoning pitting "the good" against "the bad," "essentialism" against "anti-essentialism," "Eurocentrism" against "anti-Eurocentrism," and so on. The endwork of such a critical task that freely places blame or adjudicates value for the sake of a castigation or rejection of worth is performed too quickly and easily. Its decisions are rendered by and appeal to the dictates of a universalist conception of "reason" and its demotic (and not at all democratic) corollary of "common sense" to construct the ideologico-conceptual grounds of what is "good" and what is "bad." The metaphysical value of this ethic of perception and its monological model of representation determines the non-oppositional grounds of truth. Conditional and definitive limits thereby demarcate the freedom of what it is possible to know and to think and what it is possible to say without offending the much guarded sensibilities of "reason" as the ideals of commonly held responses to cultural institutions and practices. Difference is abdicated in favor of a community of shared interpretative responsibility and the unethical hegemony of its "majority rules" attitude that bids one to erect barriers against diversity.

A more productive approach would open up the possibility of reaffirming the utility and necessity of UNESCO as a cosmopolitical institution by recontextualizing the conditions of its founding to the "new situation" ("Des humanités," Derrida, 1996: 3) of the present day. But with a vigilant questioning of its logic of practice. Derrida has provided a way to begin reassessing and reaffirming the responsibilities of UNESCO in relation to the demands and conditions of a "new international" by opening up the logic of its existence as a "world institution" concerned with the problem of global education to the question of human rights. Derrida does not call for an uncritical rejection of the memory of the institution to avoid the consequences of what Kant feared most: the danger of a non- or anti-philosophical development of human being and its institutions resulting in conceptual assimilation and ideological totality. A disturbing implication follows as it foreshadows the classical divisions of Eurocentrism by distinguishing those who are perceived to have civilization and those who supposedly do not. Kant identifies the Occidentalism of a cosmopolitical trajectory. One that "first of all tak[es] this history in its Greek, and then Roman, beginnings—in opposition to the so-called barbaric nations" ("Of the Humanities and the Philosophical Discipline," Derrida, 1996: 3). A "convenient instrument of representation [*Darstellung*]" (ibid.: 3), Derrida calls it, this binary depiction of human being. The affective influence of its trace demarcates and legitimizes the general culture of a Western subjectivity as the only "authentic" mode of being-in-the-world, distinct from and a priori to its alien Others. "This is why," Derrida stresses,

> this text [of Kant's] which is cosmopolitical in spirit, according to a law that could be verified well beyond Kant, is the most strongly Eurocentered text that can be, not only in its philosophical axiomatic but also in its retrospective reference to Greco-Roman history and its prospective reference to the future hegemony of Europe which, Kant says, is the continent that "will probably legislate some day for all others."

> (ibid.: 3)

UNESCO cannot be viewed simply as a political *organon* that represents and wields the interests and power of a Western intellectual imperialism obsessed with promoting the archival essence of itself at the expense of an Other as part of the axiomatics and axiology of its governing charter. This negative aspect of its institutional history and historicity cannot be denied, given its Eurocentric response and responsibility, the "rational ruse"(ibid.: 3) of its origins as a union of nations, states, and peoples of "equal partnership" but of unequal participation, voice, power, and representation.

INSTITUTIONS, PHILOSOPHY, AND HISTORICAL MEMORY

The ethical impetus of deconstruction begins with a philosophical nod to what is, for Derrida, the performative legacy of the institutions and models of "Greco-European memory" ("Of the Humanities and the Philosophical Discipline," Derrida, 1996: 4). Addressing the textual composition of this epistemic and cultural genealogy of Western knowledge, Kant's discourse is only one example of a host of writings by philosophers who possess the temerity to have made such audacious and largely accurate statements about the dominance of "the guiding thread [*Leitfaden*] of Greek history [*griechische Geschichte*]" (ibid.: 3), with respect to explaining the unfolding of the Reason of Being across space and over time. The axiomaticity of this logic directed at excluding an "Other" from the fundamental (pure) archive of its heritage would only be "natural" from a philosophical perspective of human historicity that narcotizes the productive value of difference and thus denies the validity of allowing for the possibility of a heterogeneous opening to a world community from a cosmopolitical point of view. As Derrida explains, "One encounters [its Eurocentric axiology] again and again, intact and invariable throughout variations as serious as those that distinguish Hegel, Husserl, Heidegger, and Valéry" (ibid.: 3). But of course there is a difference in what Kant proposes by way of a vision of the world from a cosmopolitical point of view and its universal enactment in the form of a "Society of Nations" despite the emphasis he places upon Greek philosophy and history. Because it attempts to sublate, to synthesize and at the same time keep, the tensions of the values of cultural difference in an amicable and moral unification of humanity worked out, more or less, along with the trajectory of the "teleological axis of this discourse [that] has become the tradition of European modernity" (ibid.: 3). The concept of nature, and specifically the "unsociability [*Ungeselligkeit, Unvertragsamkeit*]"[5] of the human being by nature, is actually the means to a salvation "through culture, art and artifice [Kunst], and reason, to make the seeds of nature grow" ("Of the Humanities and the Philosophical Discipline," Derrida, 1996: 3). And Kant truly believes in the potentially unifying power of this "natural or originary state of war among men" (ibid.: 3) (again Derrida's word, and it is quite appropriate here, for in Kant's time there could literally only be a state of war among men). Violence—and its threat to the security of human *Dasein*—are the catalyst that allows nature "to aid reason and thereby put philosophy into operation through the society of nations" (ibid.: 3). This is a troubling thesis, holding together the logic of the cosmopolitical community of global proportions around the concept of conflicting alterity as a productive tension for peace. On the one hand, peace achieved through the danger of violence is not really a peace made at all. It is a provisional state of human entropy with respect to the appeasement of the tensions of difference and the possible uprising of transgressions and aggressions against subjective alterity that depends on the ethico-philosophical essence of the cosmopolitical covenant of being. The condition of peace represents the satiating of a reaction to nullify the difference of difference. On the other, a peace compelled by the dark side of the human spirit is perhaps the only possible and natural peace that could be rendered effective or legislated under circumstances within which no other decision or action is acceptable, viable, or defensible given the alternative of violence. This of course begs the question of the constitutive force of community—whatever that IDEAL may entail as an affective identification of a subjective sense of belonging, a being-at-home-in-the-world WITH OTHERS—and the responsibility of its opening-up of the Self unto the difference of the Other. When these two states or conditions of existence, peace (community) and violence (war), are placed in direct opposition to each other, the ethical choice is clearly delineated by the power of a humanistic appeal that is made to a universal and hence moral will denying the propriety of any transgression of subjectivity at all costs. Even if this means suppressing human rights and freedoms for an imperative of "the greater good." Community, then, is a matter of instilling and practicing a homogeneous concept of culture, a general culture whose model of a collective intersubjectivity acts as a unified resistance to the threat of alterity. The promoting of common points of recognition and identification within the ideologico-philosophical consciousness of its constituents in order to defy or suppress the propensity for violence against the threat of difference—or at the very least to quell the performativity of the desire to do so—establishes the psychic and figural ground for the foundations of friendship and belonging. Playing by the determinative ethics of these rules of consensus in the name of community and commonality, and also of communication, reduces the Other to the Same and minimizes the potential of a subjective resistance to the inclusion of contrariety within the sphere of a closed system of shared associations. This illusion of unity masks the radical violence of alterity and softens the risk of its provisional acceptance by replacing the shock of its reality with the comforting image of a single, harmonious group, a majority without difference. They is Us. The correlation of subjectivity relieves the discord of diversity because one has to inhere and adhere to the fundamental agreements of a consensual state of abstract universalism to be part of the general yet specific culture of a community. I am We.

An ethical and philosophical contrition of sorts must be achieved in this case by the subject to ensure the manifestation of a "responsible response" that is itself a coming to peace of the Self with the (un)avowable laws of a community and its effacing of difference. If we consider the Eurocentrism of the reasoning Kant puts forward for pursuing a universal alliance of humanity from the cosmopolitical view, and its prefiguring of new models of global gathering and world institutions like the United Nations and UNESCO, we cannot avoid addressing the ethico-philosophical focus of such an idea aimed at re-articulating the notion of community. The appeal made to the "higher value" and "intrinsic right" of "Greek historicity or historiographicity" (ibid.: 3) is an attempt to formalize the vision of the endless progression of being toward its positive ethical articulation in "the good life." Again, the subsumption of all humanity under the ideological framework of institutions that are the product of a West European historicity cannot be an innocent and happy coincidence. The Eurocentrism of the utopia that Kant champions also predicts the creation of organizations such as UNESCO, for example, because the philosophical enactment of its promise for a state of lasting peace is what motivates the impossible achievement of persuading its members to a nonviolent surrendering of their individual autonomy to the security of the collective, essentially by "contracting artificial and institutional links, and into entering a

Society of Nations" (ibid.: 3). Even so, the question cannot but remain: Why? What privileges Greek history—"history both in the sense of *Geschichte* and *histoire*, history in the sense of event and of narrative, of the authenticated account, of historical science" (ibid.: 3)—to mediate and guide the future of a cosmopolitical unification of all humanity? The argument brings us, to what is called "philosophy" and "who" has a right to it, why, where, in what place; the question of the right to philosophy is also a question of the right philosophy.

FROM THE RIGHT TO PHILOSOPHY TO THE COSMOPOLITICAL VIA DECONSTRUCTION

If an institution—and this word takes in philosophy, imbibes and performs it—is true to its constitution and its name, it must allow for the opportunity to inaugurate something "new" out of its ground, the undying memory of "the old," to repeat the ethico-political performance of its founding contract and its obligations to honor the legitimacy of the Other in an affirmative way, "to criticize, to transform, to open the institution to its own future"(Caputo, 1997: 6). Derrida explains:

> The paradox in the instituting moment of an institution is that, at the same time that it starts something new, it also continues something, is true to the memory of the past, to a heritage, to something we receive from the past, from our predecessors, from the culture. If an institution is to be an institution, it must to some extent break with the past, keep the memory of the past while inaugurating something absolutely new ... So the paradox is that the instituting moment in an institution is violent in a way, violent because it has no guarantee. Although it follows the premises of the past, it starts something absolutely new, and this newness, this novelty, is a risk, is something that has to be risky, and it is violent because it is guaranteed by no previous rules. So, at the same time, you have to follow the rule and to invent a new rule, a new norm, a new criterion, a new law. That's why the moment of institution is so danger-ous at the same time. One should not have an absolute guarantee, an absolute norm; we have to invent the rules.[6]

Deconstruction welcomes the risk to participate fully in the awkward tensions between the conservation and violence of this moment of institution and the originality or newness that it produces. It embraces the opportunity to go where it cannot go and to usher in the impossibility of experiencing an other heading by pushing the limits of what is beyond the predictability of the possible.

> That is what deconstruction is made of: not the mixture but the tension between memory, fidelity, the preservation of something that has been given to us, and, at the same time, heterogeneity, something new,

and a break. The condition of this performative success, which is never guaranteed, is the alliance of these to newness.[7]

Deconstruction enacts, in itself and for itself, in the name of being responsible, just, to the alterity of the Other, an affirmation of the difference of the wholly other [tout autre], by mobilizing and navigating the tensions between (1) what is undeconstructible, unforeseeable, à venir, to come, and (2) what is deconstructible, the rule of law, its structural security and the foundation itself, so as to create the conditions for initiating something new. And this leads us back to the question of space and place, of disciplinarity and democracy, and the problem of determining who has the right to education, who has the right to philosophy. Not an easy task, as we will see.

So, is the question "of the right to philosophy" also a question of democracy and of the right of all to participate in the curricular orientation of a "public education" for peace?

The question of the right to philosophy is precisely a question of democracy and of the validity of its systems of governance, of which the institution of pedagogy is a vital element of its inner and outer workings. For, we well know that public education initially began as a way to educate the subject into citizenhood by legislating the ways of the State and its interpretative judicature into the experience of schooling. Leaving the unlettered innocence of childhood behind has historically meant becoming a "responsible member of society," defined via a liberal utilitarian concept of functional literacy as the ability one has to read and thus adhere to the letter of the law. To be more specific, then, the idea of willfully exercising the right one possesses to teach and learn, in moving from the study of rights to that of philosophy, for Derrida constitutes the initial step taken toward realizing the historico-conceptual groundwork for the immanent reality of the institution of education in a "democracy to come." What would it look like? What would it imply for the right to philosophy? For pedagogy?

Its instauration would be empowering. That is, its ethic of practice would take into account the right to philosophy and the formations of subjectivity from a cosmopolitical point of view by addressing "the competition among several philosophical models, styles and traditions that are linked to national or linguistic histories, even if they can never be reduced to effects of a nation or a language" ("Of the Humanities and the Philosophical Discipline," Derrida, 1996: 4). Here, Derrida gives a specific example of the directions of a possible heading that can be explored further:

> To take the most canonical example, which is far from being the only one and which itself includes numerous sub-varieties, the opposition between the so-called continental tradition of philosophy and the so-called analytic or Anglo-Saxon philosophy is not reducible to national limits or linguistic givens. This is not only an immense problem and an enigma for European or Anglo-American philosophers who have been trained in these such

traditions. A certain history, notable but not only a colonial history, constituted these two models as hegemonic references in the entire world. The right to philosophy requires not only an appropriation of these two competing models and of almost every other model by all, men and women (par tous et par toutes, and when I say toutes, it is not so as to be prudent regarding grammatical categories ...), the right of all (men and women) to philosophy also requires the reflection, the displacement and the deconstruction of these hegemonies, the access to places and philosophical events which are exhausted neither in these two dominant traditions nor in these languages. The stakes are already intra-European.

(ibid.: 4)

Exercising the right to philosophy from the cosmopolitical point of view would not be the result of any politicized determination of a revolutionary movement or populist gathering or theoretical trend intended to reclaim control of subjective agency. Or to wrestle the freedom over thought and thinking, back from the modus organum of the intellectual apparatus of "the State"—the educational system—in order to render it unto a nameless, faceless, sexless, and ultimately indistinguishable mass of humanity so endearingly called "the people." This is no route to a contemporary rethinking of the "concepts of state, of sovereignty" ("Des humanités," Derrida, 1996: 3) in relation to the struggles of actualizing the differences of a new global community as we are experiencing them today. For the efforts undertaken to install the hegemony of an empirico-philosophical ground to "rationalize" a new structurality of governance, no matter how "egalitarian" or "democratic" in principle, would be haunted by the living ghosts of resentful memories that would no doubt shape the future of a "democracy to come" in a highly reactionary way by limiting its conditional possibility to a negative determination of the moment of institution.

The simple (thoughtless) act of reinstitution unwittingly repeats the appropriatary logic of the hierarchy and re-enacts a litany of exclusionary injunctions, both consciously and unconsciously, whether it wants to or not, across the cultural border wars of what constitutes a welcoming of the right to philosophy from the cosmopolitical point of view to recognize an other that constitutes us. It would make absolutely no sense to attempt to level an institution, to want to (if indeed one ever could) bring its efficacy to a standstill and make its existence superfluous or an anachronism. Even though, on the surface at least, the material formation of its regulative idea and operative ideal may seem to be a system quite closed unto the reality of itself, and devoid of any space through which to achieve a productive opening to alterity. Deconstruction is not Destruction [Abbau], however. A counterresistance to the conditions and effects of institutionality must maintain and occupy the discursive form of an intractable questioning that always already takes place from within the language practices of the institution but at the outer periphery of its limits.

A question of the right to philosophy [du droit à la philosophie] and of the right philosophy is one that must interrogate the "how" and the "why" of justifying the assignation of privilege over a domain of knowledge and its institution within the university to a governing body that is thereby given power to instruct and dictate a judgment claiming, more or less, the force of law regarding the future destination of a discipline and who may or may not have access to it. The intermingling of language with power to augment or repress voice is nothing new. It has always existed to reinforce the act of institution by fusing the constative and performative functions of speech to legitimize the seriousness of the scene of founding and all that it signifies as the reproduction of the reconstitution of a body of knowledge into a material form of praxis.

The illusion of newness enters the world in this familiar way via the difference of the repetition of what is old. And here "the appropriation but also the surpassing of languages" ("Of the Humanities and the Philosophical Discipline," Derrida, 1996: 4) brings back the element of cultural memory in philosophy as that which foresees, on the one hand, "the phenomena of dogmatism and authority" (ibid.: 4) established by the linking of the past to the construction of a universal public knowledge and, on the other, "paths that are not simply anamnesic, in language which are without filiational relation to these roots" (ibid.: 4).

The right of institution accentuates the imperative to control the lines of communication. To make reasons make sense without recourse to the contrariety and complementarity of the arguments of an "other side." The "trick" of a deconstructive defiance to this effect of etiologizing, however, is to insert oneself within the openings of the system, at the periphery, its margins, where its center breaks down, fissures and cracks, welcomes heterogeneity and difference. "With a sole language [the global extension of English as an international language is the example Derrida uses], it is always a philosophy, an axiomatic of philosophical discourse and communication, which imposes itself without any possible discussion" (ibid.: 4). By not preserving, at the very least, the "due process" of an open and public discussion on matters "educational," and for our purposes "philosophical" also, then justice is not served, is not accounted for, and is thus not seen as being served with respect to reinforcing the socio-historical preconditions of an affirmative reconciliation of the Self with the Other in the discursive arena of the civic sphere. Something that is a necessary and integral feature of the legal and ethical outworkings of a participatory democracy. To be more precise. When one individual or group has, is given, or takes all but total control of the constructible field of public knowledge (e.g., the institution of pedagogy) and has discreet power over the conditions of its material/cultural dissemination (e.g., a curriculum defines and models its method of teaching and learning, establishes evaluative criteria), then this self-limiting structure of closed governance reinforces the divisive criteria of inclusion and exclusion that make any decisions regarding public education void of any sense of responsibility and respectful response to the alterity of another. Such is the power of right, and the sense of its law, for it is forcefully bestowed and exercised freely and autonomously without the necessity of providing a reason, justification or explanation.

Deconstruction counters the hegemony of a universal language and the monodimensional references of its teaching and learning by stressing the ties between philosophy and the idiomatic. The right to free thinking and its expression without fear of punishment or reprisal characterizes the democratic imperative. For Derrida, this not so obvious relationship between the everyday utility of philosophy and what it enables one to achieve in the unique contexts of an infinitely perfectable life-world is what concretizes the value of knowledge and liberates the utterance and circulation of ideas in the public sphere. It is a matter, then, of difference and of democracy, of "putting into operation each time in an original way and in a non-finite multiplicity of idioms, producing philosophical events which are neither particularistic and intranslatable nor transparently abstract and univocal in the element of an abstract universality" (ibid.: 4). A sovereign monolingualism, Derrida will contend, obliges the responsibility of a response by way of a questioning of the question, the legitimacy of its space and place:

> suppos[ing] that between the question and the place, between the question of the question and the question of the place, there be a sort of implicit contract, a supposed affinity, as if a question should always be first authorized by a place, legitimated in advance by a determined space that makes it both rightful and meaningful, thus making it possible and by the same token necessary, both legitimate and inevitable.
>
> (ibid.: 1)

Would we not expect as much of "imposing and legitimating appelations"?[8] Well, yes and no. Deconstruction would not have it any other way. Derrida poses the problem of the propriety of the question of the right to philosophy, where and how it should be asked and by whom, because he knows we cannot refuse an affirmative response to the implications of the scenario, e.g., UNESCO is "the privileged place" ("Of the Humanities and the Philosophical Discipline," Derrida, 1996: 2) for inquiring into the right of philosophy. It is a matter of reaching a "proper destination" (ibid.: 2) by navigating the journey of the mission the institution "has assigned to itself" (ibid.: 2).

Could we refuse the possibility of arriving at a cosmopolitical utopia? Could we do such a thing, reasonably support its resistance, and still be responsible to the democratic rights and principles that sanction the appearance of an institution such as UNESCO in the first place? The deconstructive "stunt" of offering impossible alternatives to choose from is one Derrida often indulges in. This one is highly rhetorical and dramatic, but not overdetermined in its effects. It defies us to simultaneously agree and disagree, by putting our assumptions temporarily under erasure so as to question the premises both of the context of the lecture and of the constitution of UNESCO, whose preamble is laced with the following words and concepts: "peace," "dignity," "democratic principles," "humanity," "justice," "liberty," "sacred duty," "mutual assistance," "perfect knowledge," "mutual understanding," "education," "culture," "war," "differences," "ignorance," "prejudice," "mutual respect," "doctrine," "inequality," "moral solidarity," "communication," and so on. Nowhere is philosophy and the right to philosophy mentioned. The constitution of UNESCO is suspiciously silent in this regard. Even though, philosophy, in every respect, structures the semantic field of the list of the words I have compiled by providing the basis for a conceptual historicity of denotations and associations relating these lexemes to ideas and the types of practices they point to. We still have free will and an open conscience, however. We can disagree at any moment with what Derrida suggests and dismiss UNESCO and its constitution as being "both too naturalist and too teleologically European" (ibid.: 5). This criticism is true enough. And UNESCO does eschew acknowledging its debt and duty to philosophy, preferring as a reactionary and "new" institution to concentrate instead on the securing of educational rights and the profusion of a scientific knowledge that champions forms of research whose intentionality is guided by and directed toward the predetermined ends its constitution spells out. A pedagogy of technological advancement becomes the chosen way to achieve economic success as a precursor to democracy and "cosmopolitical communication" (ibid.: 4). Relating to the effects of this curricular intention, Derrida has an unfulfilled "wish" about sustaining and expanding an exploration of the extent to which philosophy is "in solidarity with the movement of science in different modes" (ibid.: 4) that he expresses in the form of a deconstructive "hypothesis":

> that, while taking into account or taking charge of this progress of the sciences in the spirit of a new era of Enlightenment for the coming millennium (and in this respect I remain Kantian), a politics of the right to philosophy for all (men and women) not be only a politics of science and of technology but also a politics of thought which would yield neither to positivism nor to scientism nor to epistemology, and which would discover again, on the scale of new stakes, in its relation to science but also to religions, and also to law and to ethics, an experience which would be at once provocation or reciprocal respect but also irreducible autonomy. In this respect, the problems are always traditional and always new, whether they concern ecology, bio-ethics, artificial insemination, organ transplantation, international law, etc. They thus touch upon the concept of the proper, of property, of the relation to self and to the other within the values of subject and object, of subjectivity, of identity, of the person, i.e., all the fundamental concepts of the charters that govern international relations and institutions, such as the international law that is, in principle, supposed to regulate them.
>
> (ibid.: 4)

Derrida is acutely aware of the fact that the right to philosophy "is everywhere suffering, in Europe and elsewhere" (ibid.: 5). To address the reason of "a limit which, even though it does not always take the explicit form of prohibition or censure, nonetheless amounts to that, for the simple reason that the means for supporting teaching and research in philosophy are limited" (ibid.: 5).

The turn to "end-oriented sciences, and to techno-economic, indeed, scientifico-military imperatives" (ibid.: 5) is cultivated, sometimes rightly and sometimes wrongly, by the desire for outcomes "labelled useful, profitable, urgent" (ibid.: 5). As Derrida correctly comments, "it is not a matter of indiscriminately contesting all of these imperatives" (ibid.: 5). There is more to it, however, than a cool detachment and acceptance of this narrowed distinction between what teaching and research is needed and what is necessary "be they in the service of economy or even of military strategy" (ibid.: 5). Derrida explains:

> the more these imperatives impose themselves—and sometimes for the best reasons in the world—the more also the right to philosophy becomes increasingly urgent, irreducible, as does the call to philosophy in order to precisely think and discern, evaluate and criticize, philosophies. For they, too, are philosophies, they that, in the name of techno-economico-military positivism and according to diverse modalities, tend to reduce the field and the chances of an open and unlimited philosophy, both in its teaching and in its research, as well as in the effectiveness of its international exchanges.
>
> (ibid.: 5)

So, why shouldn't we reject the example of UNESCO and choose to re-examine the nature of its propriety to ask the question of the right to philosophy? As we enter the uncertainty of a new millennium, what does it have to offer the future of thinking beyond the economic potential and promise of a scientific and technological cosmopolitanism?

To say that UNESCO is not a legitimate institution, a "good" institution, would be to deny the good it has done or can do by ignoring its potential for an effective improvement of what—among other things—it does do well: it fights for a limitation in the reduction of access to education on a global scale. Which is to say, it has the capacity and is "duty bound," (ibid.: 4) in principle, to protect the right to philosophy from a cosmopolitical point of view, even if its constitution does not explicitly say so. And this responsibility is what foreshadows the possibility of enacting the progressive movement of joining together nations, states, and peoples in a transformational enterprise aimed at negotiating the effectivity of a democracy to come. It involves taking the risk of affirming that in "today's world the stakes have never been as serious, and they are new stakes," (ibid.: 4) whose formations call into question the very concepts defining human organizations and relations embodied in the constitution of UNESCO, what we in the West automatically accept as self-evident truths about the universal plan of nature, and its cosmopolitical democracy Kant made so much of. The violence of authority is not determinate, however. It is subtle, stratified, and discontinuous in its effects, and therefore it must be approached with a respectful skepticism, like that of deconstruction, which lies "between a certain erasure and a certain reaffirmation of debt—and sometimes a certain erasure in the name of reaffirmation" (ibid.: 5). That is, if we really want to make our way toward a philosophical reconciliation of difference and autonomy in light of the colonialist historicity of the West. For "what one calls, in Greek, democracy" (ibid.: 4) can neither stand nor do without the presence of real dissensus in its community. So, we must be careful not put philosophy "off limits." Not at all!

We must mobilize the right to philosophy in a way that would address the violence of authority in democracy by situating its ethical efficacy and validity according to "what today may constitute the limit or the crisis most shared by all the societies, be they Western or not," (ibid.: 5) as to the internal and international negotiation of their future from a cosmopolitical point of view. Again the reason for Derrida's lecture is not to safeguard the boundaries of a discipline that is always already its other. It voices the "call for a new philosophical reflection upon what democracy, and [he insists] the democracy to come, may mean and be" (ibid.: 4). The violence of authority has power to induce silences, but it does not totally restrict the interpretative engagement of consciousness. Interestingly enough, it can produce a heightening of thinking, sharpening its philosophical intensity by expanding rather than reducing the human capacity to "respond responsibly," to question the absolute right and legitimacy of knowledge, its privilege, in an ethical way by opening up the self-validating aspect of the institution to the voice of what is "Other." This is the underlying theme of the lecture. It details the importance of not abandoning the right to philosophy, its teaching and learning. For what Derrida maintains will and can happen, and what he hopes for, is a reconfiguring of democracy according to a post-Kantian view of cosmopolitanism. Through a fundamental interrogation of the ground of the reason of UNESCO, its mission in practice and in principle, deconstruction locates the transformative field of its hermeneutic constellation "among several registers of debt, between a finite debt and an infinite debt" (ibid.: 5) that articulate the space between the place of the question of philosophy, the question of the place of philosophy, and the question of the question of philosophy. That would, hence, situate the ethical impetus of its interpretative domain of the institution within the structural locality of its right to question the question of the right to philosophy as well as the nature of institution and institutionality in its relation to the cosmopolitical.

Deconstruction, we must recall, is above all affirmation. Its "yes, yes," "come, come," is a confirmation of its unconditional acceptance of the Other rooted in an infinite responsibility for and to the Other, whose deferral and difference, its différance, it faithfully protects at all costs. Without reservation or doubt. Safeguarding the possibility of the question of the right to philosophy, deconstruction heralds the impossibility of a (re)teaching of the Self to be open to a learning from the alterity of the Other. That is, its integrity is tied to its original and originary aim at raising the spirit of human perfectability through its vigilance of the ethical terms of what constitutes a just response to difference and otherness and the infinite responsibility that comes with this unprovoked and selfless affirmation of the Other.

Notes

1 See The "Roundtable Discussion," in Jacques Derrida's "Des humanités et de la discipline philosophiques"/"Of the Humanities and Philosophical Disciplines," Surfaces Vol. VI.108 (v.1.0A–16/08/1996), 1.
2 See Jacques Derrida (1990: 111–53).
3 Cited in Derrida, "Of the Humanities and the Philosophical Discipline," p. 2.
4 The "Roundtable Discussion" in Derrida (1996: 5–40) involved Hazard Adams, Ernst Behler, Hendrick Birus, Jacques Derrida, Wolfgang Iser, Ludwig Pfeiffer, Bill Readings, Ching-hsien Wang, and Pauline Yu. All further quotations from this text are comments made by Derrida. The page references are from the Web site version of the text to found at http://tornade.ere.umontreal.ca/guedon/Surfaces/vol6/derrida.html. This note refers to a quotation from page 3.
5 Immanuel Kant, cited in Derrida, "Of the Humanities and the Philosophical Discipline," 3.
6 Jacques Derrida, cited in Caputo (1997: 6).
7 Derrida, cited in ibid.: 6.
8 See Jacques Derrida (1998: 39).

References

Caputo, J. (1997). *Deconstruction in a Nutshell: Conversation with Jacques Derrida.* New York: Fordham University Press.

Derrida, J. (1990). "Où commence et comment finit un corps enseignant," in *Du droit à la philosophie*. Paris: Galileé, pp. 111–53.

——(1996). "Des humanités et de la discipline philosophiques"/"Of the Humanities and Philosophical Disciplines," Surfaces, VI.108 (v.1.0A–16/08/1996), 1.

——. (1998) *Monolingualism of the Other; or, The Prosthesis of Origin*, trans. Patrick Mensah. Stanford, CA: Stanford University Press.

6 Education for "Peace" in Urban Canadian Schools

Gender, Culture, Conflict, and Opportunities to Learn

Kathy Bickmore

School-based education for peace has had a paradoxical relationship with the realities of conflict and violence: it does not necessarily disrupt patterns of overt violence, much less the structural violence of injustice and social exclusion (Curle et al., 1974). In fact, some school practices legitimate and reinforce structural and/or overt violence, at the same time that other school practices contribute to positive peacebuilding (Bush and Saltarelli, 2000; Davies, 2004; Weinstein et al., 2007; Williams, 2004). Prevailing approaches to explicit peace education have been shaped by their origins in primarily high status populations in relatively peaceful social contexts (e.g. Bekerman and McGlynn, 2007; Lederach, 1995; Salomon and Nevo, 2002). In school practice, this may result in a disproportionate emphasis on 'negative peace'—cessation or temporary prevention of overt violence. This facilitates social stability, thus advantaging those currently in power (Galtung, 1969). 'Peacekeeping' refers to the use of coercion to achieve negative peace. In schools, this typically takes the form of monitoring and punitive discipline. However, even 'peacemaking' or conflict resolution dialogue processes, when they emphasize quick or premature settlement rather than messier democratic dialogue to build justice, may contribute more to negative peace than to transformative peacebuilding.

Curriculum is a privileged discourse that legitimates certain ways of thinking and de-legitimates others (Apple, 1990). While schools teach about conflict explicitly, through lessons and communication of rules, probably the most powerful curriculum is implicit—affirmation of particular identities and behaviors through patterns of practice, language and silences. 'Peacebuilding' means comprehensively changing the status quo, achieving a dynamic 'positive' (just and sustainable) peace by de-legitimating the beliefs and practices that normalize violence, marginalization, and oppression (Galtung, 1996). Values, wrapped up in structures of social relationships and language about social difference, shape (and are shaped by) the knowledge, communication, and interpretations that define any conflict in its cultural context (Ross, 2007). In schools, building an equitable, inclusive sense of community and facilitating repair of the harms people cause one another can build motivation, skills, and social capital (relationship resources) for constructive engagement and peacebuilding (Gladden, 2002; Harris and Morrison, 2003; Morrison, 2007).

In particular, people's learning and performance of (non)violent behavior are inextricably bound up in their gender and other cultural identities (Brock-Utne, 1989; Davies, 2004; Reardon, 1996). In varied ways across cultures and contexts, performance of 'female' identity in dominant discourses is associated with nurturing, passive, or collaborative responses to conflict. Masculinity is predominantly associated with aggression and competition. Children learn about how they are expected to manage conflicts, and about their roles and value as citizens, amidst their development as historically and geographically located female, male, sexual and cultural beings (Epstein and Johnson, 1998; Gordon et al., 2000). While both explicit and implicit curriculum often reinforce overt violence (such as war-making and gender-based harassment) and structural violence (such as entrenched enmity and injustice), they simultaneously create some spaces for challenging and alleviating such violence.

While the rhetoric of public schooling affirms democracy and social justice goals, the study described below shows that actually-implemented anti-violence and conflict resolution initiatives in certain urban Canadian schools emphasized peacekeeping and negative peace far more than democratic peacebuilding transformation. This chapter probes the implications of such 'peace' education for the reinforcement of gendered, racialized social inequalities.

IMPLICIT AND EXPLICIT CURRICULUM, CONFLICT AND DIFFERENCE IN SCHOOLS

Implicit curriculum such as discipline and 'violence prevention' often disproportionately monitors and blames visible minority and economically marginalized males, who are stereotypically assumed to be most heavily involved with violence and vandalism (Noguera, 1995). Girls who are non-disruptive are often ignored, while girls who resist aggressively may be sanctioned more harshly than boys who act similarly (Slee, 1995). At the same time, less visible kinds of violence, that disproportionately limit girls' and gender-bending boys' access to safe and complete education, such as peer exclusion and sexual harassment, are often relatively ignored by school personnel (Bergsgaard, 1997; Stein, 1995). Influenced by intersecting social identity hierarchies, each young person interacts differently, practices different roles, and draws on different personal/cultural resources and knowledge: thus even when educated together with the 'same' curriculum, diverse students are not getting the same education about conflict.

Interpersonal violence intersects with, and is exacerbated by, structural violence. Too often there is a double standard in the ways various forms of disrespect are normalized or punished. As Epp puts it:

> When we respond to violence in schools, if we respond at all, it is to the children who are violent ... When a student embarrasses, ridicules or

scorns another student it is harassment, bullying or teasing. When a teacher does it, it is [seen as] sound pedagogical practice.

(Epp and Watkinson, 1996: 20)

However, bias-based harassment flourishes in some environments far more than in others, indicating that localized understandings and practices can make a difference. For example, school climate surveys in the USA and in Nova Scotia show Black students to be more likely than students from white or other groups to believe that teachers don't respect students, that racism is a problem in their schools, and/or that they are not treated equitably (Conrad, 2006; Gewertz, 2006). Power-imbalanced social aggression (by adults or peers) is not effectively controlled by typical approaches to school discipline, which tend to focus on individual student behavior without addressing social hierarchies or structural patterns.

Effective anti-violence programs—unlike the prevailing punishment-heavy approaches—are multifaceted, inclusive, anti-discriminatory, offer learning support for teachers and students, and are sustained in frequency and duration (Catalano et al., 2002; Erickson and McGuire, 2004; Hazler and Carney, 2002; Scheckner et al., 2002). Comprehensive, long-range programming that includes both explicit instruction and regular practice in conflict management, equity, and restorative peacebuilding—both co-curricular dispute resolution and infused in classroom curriculum—have been shown to reduce aggressive behavior (and associated suspensions) and to develop participants' understanding, reasoning and social skills, and openness to handle conflict nonviolently (Bickmore, 2002; Burrell et al., 2003; Garrard and Lipsey, 2007; Harris, 2005; Heydenberk and Heydenberk, 2005; Jones, 2004; Skiba, 2000; Stevahn, 2004). It is naïve and dangerous to apply simple negotiation-based peacemaking approaches to complex social conflict and aggression: power imbalances can be reinforced, and harm compounded. However, some more complex approaches to dialogic problem-solving—such as class meetings and circle processes conducted by skilled, equity-conscious facilitators—hold substantial promise as part of a comprehensive response to complex social aggression (Morrison, 2007). Unfortunately, these characteristics do not describe the programming typically implemented in North America (e.g. Crosse et al., 2002; Jull, 2000).

Explicit, implemented North American public school curriculum generally avoids open, respectful dialogue about specific cases of conflict, dissent or controversy (Avery et al., 1999; Houser, 1996; Sears et al., 1999; Simon, 2001). Schools' culture and context often obstruct the constructive introduction of educative conflict or criticism, for example, through pressures for mandated content coverage, restricted autonomy for teachers, and lock-step school schedules (e.g. Bickmore, 2008; Little, 1993; Popkewitz, 1991). Officially, peacebuilding-related learning expectations (such as concepts of conflict, power, justice and change, skills for discussing and deliberating controversial issues) are increasingly embedded in mandated curriculum requirements across

Canada in a variety of subject areas (Bickmore, 2005a). However, public schools have very few resources to support actual implementation of such democratic, learning-centered peacebuilding education, instead spending resources on security control and on punitive responses after incidents of violence (Bickmore, 2005b). At the same time, a glance at news media or popular culture demonstrates that people find social, political, and interpersonal conflict to be fascinating and important.

Classroom knowledge is suspect in the minds/hearts of learners (not to mention boring) when it ignores the conflicts that students see and live, inside and outside school (McNeil, 1986). Conflict-avoidant curriculum shuts out the contrasting viewpoints embodied in the life experiences of young people, especially those from dominated groups (e.g. Anzaldúa, 1987; Harber, 2002). A student's repertoire of skills for handling conflict, and her confidence in applying those skills, can be expected to improve with application, elaboration, and practice. A curriculum for equitable peacebuilding, therefore, would give all youngsters opportunities to practice handling taboo topics and unsettling viewpoints, especially in relation to the complex social/political/transnational issues that are less easily learned in homes and neighborhoods.

"A liberatory pedagogy ... needs to render explicit topics that are most often relegated to realms of null curricula in many mainstream classrooms. Thus silences, omissions, controversy, and taboo subjects ... can become spaces of possibility and self-understanding" (Henry, 1994: 312–13). These uncommon pedagogies, when implemented, do significantly improve young people's capacities and intentions to engage in political life, including struggles for equity and peace (Torney-Purta et al., 2001).

It's not just controversial and sensitive issues that are avoided, but attention to the inherent locatedness and subjectivity of knowledge (Britzman, 1998; Deng and Luke, 2008). How would students learn to critique value-laden assumptions about peace and conflict, in relation to specific identities including their own, if the value-embeddedness of knowledge is never acknowledged? It's not quite fair to call the prevailing master narrative a 'male' perspective, since it represents only a small proportion of even the male population— white, heteronormative, dominant-class leaders of government and military actions, and the occasional heroic exception. Textbooks often still relegate to their margins the experiences and perspectives of women and people of color. For example, female 'firsts' in formerly male pursuits are often included, because they fit the dominant image of 'male' activity as what matters. Less-tokenizable roles of women, reflecting viewpoints conflicting with those of dominant men—for instance, in labor and human rights movements, building communities, working for peace—are noticeably absent from North American curriculum texts, even in explicit citizenship education or social studies (Baldwin and Baldwin, 1992; Hahn, 1996; McIntosh, 2005; Noddings, 1992; Woyshner, 2002).

Feminist and critical post-colonial pedagogies can open spaces for meaningful exploration of conflicts and peacebuilding options. However, in the context of social hierarchies, this depends on the creation of safer learning climates—widening the margins of accepted viewpoints, and interrogating the exclusions and discontinuities in 'democratic' life. Heteronormative boys typically have several advantages in the lived curriculum of school behavior, such as teacher attention, influential voice in discussions, and relative safety from harassment (Gordon et al., 2000; Griffin and Ouellett, 2003; Sadker, 1999; Weikel, 1995). Feminist teaching brings conflicts into open dialogue, and takes responsibility to confront bigotry and harmful behavior when it does occur (hooks, 1994; Robinson, 2005). However, this is not without risks: conflictual pedagogy can silence or exclude at the same time that it generates interest (Ellsworth, 1989). When even a skilled teacher engages 'the class' in analysis or discussion of divergent and challenging viewpoints, usually only some of the highest-status students are practicing some semblance of democratic conflict dialogue, while other students remain implicitly excluded, withdrawn into the temporary safety of silence. Considering the vulnerability of young people to insecurity and peer censure, one could argue that it is unfair to expect all students to participate in conflictual pedagogy. Yet, how else would diverse students get a chance to develop confidence in voicing and substantiating their own opinions? When a timid or formerly-ignored person does speak up in a group, she helps to reshape both her self-expectations and the expectations and interests of her peers (Cohen, 1994).

In a long-term observational study of four teachers' high school social studies classes that I conducted 20 years ago, diverse students responded in widely varying ways to conflictual teaching, even in free-flowing discussions (Bickmore, 1993). While more students were generally engaged when conflicting perspectives were on the table, compared to more traditional pedagogies, more girls than boys (but some of each) still remained silent. When the conflictual topic was framed as a competitive debate, the disparity between the 'stars' and the 'silent majority' was even bigger. Girls and low-status students are somehow taught, implicitly if not explicitly, that to be outspoken is not academically relevant, not polite, even trouble-making.

Jarred by related research findings about gender socialization in their own school, some teachers were provoked to re-consider their own unconscious modeling and perpetuation of 'good girl' manners:

> Unless we stopped hiding in expectations of goodness and control, our behavior would silence any words to girls about speaking in their own voice. Finally, we dared to believe that one could be intelligently disruptive without destroying anything except the myths about the high level of female cooperativeness.
>
> (Gilligan and Brown, 1992: 221)

Thus, given support and opportunities for their own critical dialogue, teachers can un-learn their perpetuation of docility and conflict avoidance in classrooms (see also Bickmore, 2005b).

Even when all are involved in well-facilitated, sincere efforts to listen across difference, unconscious assumptions (and the demands of 'knowledge acquisition' in academic contexts) can inadvertently silence unpopular voices, reinforcing participants' prior locations in the social hierarchy (Bickford, 1996). In contrast, Ellsworth proposes a "different ethic:"

> It's an ethic committed to conflict without, paradoxically, needing the idea of an enemy. It is an ethic that operates not within the logic of oppositions and mutual exclusions, but within the logic of paradoxes and spectrums ... [This pedagogy] manipulates us into a fluid positioning that sees back and forth across boundaries, and as a result, requires us to take on responsibility for the meanings we will construct.
>
> (Ellsworth, 1989: 319)

Such feminist poststructural perspectives point to ways teachers might facilitate learning opportunities that embrace and encourage paradoxical coexistences and multiple viewpoints (see also Kumashiro, 2000, 2004).

In this global society, however, interpersonal openness and participation are clearly not sufficient for peacebuilding. The precious and fragile core of democratic peacebuilding is citizen action to influence collective decision-making and governance, in the context of continuing social conflict (Franklin, 2006). The people excluded from formal democratic procedures for generations, including women, have frequently engaged in political action—exerting influence on their own and others' behalf—even when their participation was explicitly disallowed within formal structures (Dietz, 1989). Participating in such democratic action, even within the coercive environment of the school, can open up new understandings about the anatomy of conflict and fragile peace, and how to influence the social institutions that create our collective future. Thus, the remainder of this chapter examines the primarily-implicit curriculum of actual practices in selected public schools, to discern the potential opportunities for diverse students to participate in conflict learning on a daily basis.

ANTI-VIOLENCE AND PRO-PEACE EDUCATIONAL ACTIVITIES IN PRACTICE

To illustrate the character and implications of peace/conflict learning initiatives actually implemented in public schools, in the context of social inequality, the remainder of this chapter draws upon a multi-year, qualitative study I recently completed. Its goal was to understand the intersections among various anti-violence, conflict resolution, and peacebuilding education policies and learning activities, at diverse schools, in urban Canadian schools with diverse student populations. Here I draw primarily on open-ended interviews with diverse staff in one large school district, with occasional reference to two comparison districts, informed by analysis of school and government documents in each city. Interviewees were key participants in a continuum of conflict-related (implicit or explicit curriculum) activities. In Board A, there were a total of 52 interviewees; 34 of these were in five focus schools (two high schools and three elementary) all with relatively transient populations of ethnically diverse students, low household incomes, and high proportions of recent immigrants, English-language learners. These particular schools were selected because their divergent suspension and expulsion rates indicated different experiences with managing student conflict and violence. Some 13 interviewees in Board A were centrally-assigned, and five led exemplary peacemaking-related programs in non-focus schools. The Boards B and C comparison studies include 21 and 18 interviews respectively, with similar proportions of school-based, centrally-assigned, and provincial staff, but no focus schools. Participants were invited to describe programs, procedures, and activities they considered relevant to peacekeeping (security measures, interventions for problem behaviors); peacemaking (conflict resolution); and/or peacebuilding (conflict resolution and equity education for students and staff, dialogue about contentious issues, structures to strengthen participation and relationships).

Most interviewees expressed uncertainty, dissent, and concern about existing approaches to handling aggression and conflict. To different degrees in different schools and boards, interviewees reported that certain populations of students, already living under challenging life circumstances, were disproportionately punished and excluded from school by implemented discipline policies. Males, especially non-affluent visible minorities (African-heritage, immigrants from West Asia, and aboriginal), were the students most often punished with suspension and expulsion.

Virtually all the 91 educators interviewed for this study expressed the belief that school staffs have a responsibility to communicate explicitly the non-violent behaviour norms they want students to exhibit. Many elementary schools approached this goal through so-called character education programs, in which adult staff were to "catch students being good," and then gave individual students public recognition and other extrinsic rewards (such as tickets toward a treat) for 'good' behavior. Such programs may indoctrinate culturally-dominant values and compliant behaviors in an uncritical manner (Otten, 2000). Sometimes girls and boys, or students of various ethnic origins, seemed to be rewarded in ways that reinforced stereotypes. These programs could affirm students' anti-violence actions, such as supporting peers rather than being passive bystanders, but they were unlikely to recognize or address subtle (gendered) relational aggression. Co-curricular extrinsic reward programs such as these are often initiated, not because they are known to be effective, but because they are easy to implement without resources for professional development.

Given scarce funding to release teachers for in-service professional development and planning, a common strategy to address social skill development was to bring in packaged programs, kits, and/or outside presenters. Several staff (especially at the most conflict-stressed schools) articulated remarkable faith and hope that they might find a particular program that would help fix their school's problems. Others, like this principal, reflected that developing peaceful classroom and school climates was not "so much [particular program] resources as a mindset, and strategies that can be shared ... by teachers sitting down together in dialogue. But the time is really scarce for that." A few social skills package programs, primarily produced by American companies for elementary classrooms, were well-known across each school board. Schools often switched packages, seeking a program that various staff would find workable and really implement in multiple grades. Most of these programs offered little or no staff support for program development, nor follow-up, thus programs were neither fully implemented nor sustained. Kits that did not include teacher training were a moderate expense, but this limited the extent to which teachers actually learned new pedagogies, much less adapted materials to suit the cultures and conflict dynamics of their particular students. Even comprehensively-implemented social skills or conflict resolution programs would not be sufficient to handle patterns of bias-based social aggression. Their emphasis on compliance with authority and dominant cultural norms can be seen as a gentle form of peacekeeping. At the same time, clearly social competence and relationship development are components of peacebuilding.

Many interviewees, especially in Boards A and B, reported a change in priorities, toward relatively controlling approaches focused on 'anti-bullying' and discipline—away from peer peacemaking education, community-building, and opportunities for student agency. Yet what clearly distinguished the focus schools that were handling conflict relatively peacefully from those with high violence and suspension rates was the quantity and variety of options for active student participation and student leadership. One high school had a remarkable range of autonomous student affinity and activity groups, facilitated by an active student council. Students there held various helper roles such as mentoring immigrant newcomers or assisting with first aid and safety. The principal met with rotating groups of about 10 diverse students per month, which resulted in tangible initiatives such as staff volunteers opening the gym for students to play lunchtime basketball in exchange for improved class attendance. Also in two of the elementary schools, diverse students were recruited for various leadership roles, such as helping at a track and field day. In contrast, in the focus elementary and high school with higher suspension rates, student leadership activity was minimal and restricted to compliant students.

Cuts in Board A's staffing over the past dozen years had caused the demise of many student peacemaking leadership programs. Participants described peer peacemaking leadership programs that, if they still existed, did not as successfully engage diverse students as they had in the past, when they were supported by dedicated human resources such as release periods and/or assistance from centrally-assigned staff. This illustrates (in the breach) the findings of research (cited above) on what makes such conflict resolution education programs effective, equitable and sustainable.

One focus elementary school had maintained for years a peer monitoring program that the principal described as "something like peacemakers." These were high-status students from the school's oldest grade, selected by teachers and administrators who viewed them as cooperative, 'positive' leaders. The teacher advisor for the program explained that prefects were "looked up to as role models and safety monitors for the other students." Once trained, they served in pairs during recesses, before and after school—reminding students to take turns, take hats off when entering the building, and so forth. Clearly these student leaders were not representative of the school's diverse population. They did far more enforcing of rules (peacekeeping) than facilitating of autonomous peer problem-solving negotiations (peacemaking). At the same time, they were clearly admired by peers (many wanted to become prefects), and performed a service that was supported enthusiastically by all the CES staff interviewed. Aronson (2000) cautions that empowerment of a few students by adults in a school could have unintended negative consequences for marginalized students, since the elevation of some in a hierarchy (with limited space at the top) consequently demotes others.

In a small number of Board A high schools, selected students were allowed to receive guidance credit, and therefore dedicated meeting time and staffing, for a one semester peacemaking-related peer leadership "GPP" course. In AHS, about 20–24 students, nominated by staff, were taught by a designated teacher, with no specific training but assistance from an outside agency. The teacher advisor explained:

> We train them (in the first four weeks of the term)—team building, communication, and so on. Then they learn to do peer mediation, anti-bullying and conflict resolution and [they] begin to do that peer leadership in the school ... A great deal of the time is spent discussing what's going on in the school. The students are very open and candid about [things like] bullying and who the loners are—stuff I wouldn't know about otherwise.

Nearly all the students selected were girls, few or none of whom had poor marks or histories of non-compliant behavior. The designated teacher had found it difficult to sustain the program, so only a few mediations and about three class presentations actually occurred.

A similar course at another Board A high school, in contrast, engaged a more diverse set of student leaders in more active leadership. A few sections of this course were offered there each year, including students self-nominated or nominated by teachers based on both 'negative' and 'positive' leadership qualities. The guidance teacher described their focus on oral and written communication skills and discussion:

We do active listening and roadblocks and I messages, assertiveness training, conflict resolution and leadership skills training—all of these components include a literacy piece ... The focus of the course is to talk about personal issues and how to be helpful with their peers ... The filling of the groups is not difficult, although it's the girls that want it much more than the guys. I have to talk some of the guys into it. The groups average about a quarter males.

Out of the concurrent GPP classes, about 12 students per year, reflecting the gender and ethnic diversity of the student body, were invited to become peer mediators. An additional full day of training built on the conflict resolution education already delivered in the course. This program had been sustained for at least ten years, offering conflict mediation upon referral by administrators, teachers, and directly from peers. While serious social aggression conflicts were not mediated by these students, the larger GPP classes from which the mediators were drawn offered a consistent, facilitated space for such matters to be discussed.

Opportunities for leadership by diverse students required solid, well-prepared, sustained adult support for programs and especially for marginalized students' development. The prefect monitor program at CES and the peer mediation program at CRE HS1 were built into each school's timetable, professional development and staffing, so that qualified adults were available to mentor diverse student leaders to carry out well-defined tasks. At AHS, a miscellany of unsustained resources had been applied to start the mediation program, and current staff did not understand the role of the student helpers. Without development of capacity within existing staff, they had been unable to develop a coherent or sustainable program.

A different kind of initiative emphasizing student peacebuilding agency was support and advocacy groups, engaging particular populations of minority or marginalized students. These groups provided a space, and support from peers and adult advisors, for students (who otherwise had been excluded and/or harassed) to develop skills, confidence, a secure sense of identity, and social relationships they could rely on to make their school experience more positively peaceful. From this base of support, some of these groups also initiated broader awareness and justice advocacy activities. The more peaceful focus school, BHS, had several such groups, many focusing on ethnic or religious affinities. At AHS, a social worker from a community agency facilitated a 'be yourself' support group—originally proposed as a Gay Straight Alliance, but the school's administration had not allowed the group name or mandate to mention homosexuality.

Anti-violence peer leadership programs, especially in Board A, tended to be small, involving few students and often marginal to the core activities of schools such as classroom curriculum. This co-curricular marginality made these opportunities inaccessible to many students who could have benefited, and could have consequently contributed more to building peaceful school communities. At the same time, the focused, co-curricular nature of these programs allowed some such initiatives to have, according to interviewees, remarkably positive effects on their few participants.

Study participants understood, of course, that much more comprehensive support for on-going, integrated school programming was needed, but felt that existing resource priorities did not allow them to make that commitment. A centrally-assigned safe schools administrator explained:

> There's no time for the more relationship-based program development ...
> I don't think we have any system plan for doing proactive and long-term
> [peacemaking education or violence prevention] ... Safety in itself won't
> make a school effective ... It's not as simple as putting Tribes into school
> A: That's not the fix, though it might be a support. We don't have the
> staff to make that happen.

A wide range of interviewees in all three districts agreed that peacemaking education with sufficient depth, breadth, meaning, and sustainability would require more equitable and effective system-wide dissemination of resource information, and dedicated staff support for school-level change.

To adequately and sustainably deal with the complex social challenges at the roots of social conflict requires (re)building healthy, reliable, inclusive and equitable relationships that are embedded in the regularized business of living together. In schools, this means changes in core activities—curriculum and pedagogy (academic and explicit as well as lived and implicit) and human relationships, especially between teachers and students. Of course, no change this major can happen all at once: The programs and practices described above each represent places where schools might begin the transformation process. When the difficult long-term goals of building inclusive, just, healthy relationships become obscured by the minutia scratching the surface of daily school life, schools retain self-sustaining patterns of coping with surface conflagrations and never getting to their sources.

Some teachers did carry out conflict resolution, bullying awareness, cross-cultural and anti-discriminatory learning activities in their classrooms, although most teachers interviewed seemed unaware that these kinds of peace-related education were, in fact, built into official curriculum requirements. Even without addressing contested issues, communication, handling multiple viewpoints, and problem-solving are basic to essentially every area of learning. For example, some elementary teachers held class meetings or circles regularly, to model and facilitate constructive communication and collective problem solving. English teachers taught conflict communication and dialogue skills, and practiced them through discussion of controversial issues, debate, and role playing. A social sciences teacher addressed issues of political conflict and cultural difference, including an oral history assignment in which students interviewed peers who were recent immigrants from origins different from their own. A health teacher spent substantial time on conflict resolution and bullying awareness. A few centrally-assigned curriculum leaders sometimes infused conflicting perspectives, justice issues, and conflict communication skills into their academic support resources for teachers. At the same time, there were minimal provincial or board resources available for pro-active curriculum leadership or teacher support.

In-depth diversity and equity education was rare in the regularized, sustained curriculum or co-curriculum in the schools in this study. Even where issues of violence and bullying were addressed, the problems of bias that so often motivate or exacerbate aggression were barely mentioned. One high school teacher advocated equity education as a key element of peacebuilding:

> I think that a good 50–60% of the conflicts [in this school] have an equity element—either race, religion, sexuality, or sexism. There is tension that a student holds in after hearing an oppressive comment, and then eventually they explode … Anytime you can facilitate equity in a school, you are facilitating peace in general, because you are facilitating acceptance and appreciation.

Clearly, such peacebuilding education requires resources, in order to eventually change schools sufficiently to reallocate resources from peacekeeping control and post-incident coping toward more proactive, humane and effective facilitation of conflict-related learning and development of healthy relationships. In educators' enthusiasm to try to reduce bullying and other aggressive behavior, the balance, especially at Board A, had tipped toward labor-intensive, painful post-incident reaction and attempts at control, away from on-going developmental education that would provide opportunities for diverse students to learn and to contribute. The interviewees in this study pointed to many spaces of possibility, none of them close to fruition.

CONCLUSION

Life revolves around conflicts and identities—disagreements, problems, decisions, injustices, clashing perspectives or interests—in any cultural context. Violence can be a symptom of underlying conflicts, and a way of handling conflicts, but it is not inevitable. The nonviolent confrontation of such conflicts is what sustains both democratic civil society and human relationships. Like oxygen, conflict can be explosive—but it is inescapable and essential to life. Unfortunately, typical urban public schools in Canada today do not embrace such conflicts as opportunities for learning and collectively creating dynamic peace. On the contrary, despite many notable shining exceptions, these schools seem much more often to ignore or actively repress expressions of difference in both implicit and explicit curriculum, focusing their efforts on achieving negative peace through control and conformity. It is a huge challenge that any peace education effort in public schools must operate in the context of this hegemonic patriarchal structure, while possibly trying to transform it from within.

References

Anzaldúa, G. (1987). *Borderlands/La Frontera: The new mestiza*. San Francisco: Spinsters/ Aunt Lute.

Apple, M. W. (1990). *Ideology and Curriculum* (2nd ed.). New York: Routledge.

Aronson, E. (2000). *Nobody Left to Hate: Teaching compassion after Columbine*. New York: Worth Publishers.

Avery, P., Johnson, D, and Johnson, R. (1999). "Teaching an Understanding of War and Peace through Structured Academic Controversies," in A. Raviv et al. (Eds.), *How Children Understand War and Peace*. San Francisco: Jossey-Bass, pp. 260–80.

Baldwin, P. and Baldwin, D. (1992). "The Portrayal of Women in Classroom Textbooks," Canadian Social Studies, 26(3), 110–14.

Bekerman, Z. and McGlynn, C. (Eds.). (2007). *Addressing Ethnic Conflict through Peace Education: International perspectives*. Basingstoke: Palgrave Macmillan.

Bergsgaard, M. (1997). "Gender Issues in the Implementation and Evaluation of a Violence-Prevention Curriculum," Canadian Journal of Education, 22(1), 33–45.

Bickford, S. (1996). *The Dissonance of Democracy*. Ithaca, NY: Cornell University Press.

Bickmore, K. (1993). "Learning Inclusion/Inclusion in Learning: Citizenship Education for a Pluralistic Society," Theory and Research in Social Education, 21(4), 341–84.

——(2002). "Peer Mediation Training and Program Implementation in Elementary Schools: Research Results," Conflict Resolution Quarterly, 19(4), 327–48.

——(2005a). "Foundations for Peacebuilding and Discursive Peacekeeping: Infusion and Exclusion of Conflict in Canadian Public School Curricula," Journal of Peace Education, 2(2), 161–81.

——(2005b). "Teacher Development for Conflict Participation: Facilitating Learning for 'Difficult Citizenship' Education," International Journal of Citizenship and Teacher Education, 1(2). Available at: www.citized.info.

——(2008). "Peace and Conflict," in J. Arthur, I. Davies and C. Hahn (Eds.), *Sage Handbook of Education for Citizenship and Democracy*. London: Sage, pp. 438–54.

Britzman, D. (1998). "Queer Pedagogy and its Strange Techniques," in D. Britzman (Ed.), *Lost Subjects, Contested Objects*. New York: SUNY Press, pp. 79–95.

Brock-Utne, B. (1989). *Feminist Perspectives on Peace and Peace Education*. Oxford: Pergamon Press.

Burrell, N., Zirbel, C., and Allen, M. (2003). "Evaluating Peer Mediation Outcomes in Educational Settings: A Meta-analytic Review," Conflict Resolution Quarterly, 21 (1), 7–26.

Bush, K. and Saltarelli, D. (2000). *The Two Faces of Education in Ethnic Conflict: Towards a peacebuilding education for children*. Florence: UNICEF Innocenti Research Centre.

Catalano, R., Berglund, M. L., Ryan, J., Lonczak, H., and Hawkins, J. D. (2002). "Positive Youth Development in the United States: Research Findings on Evaluations of Positive Youth Development Programs," Prevention and Treatment, 5, article 15. Available at: www.psycinfo.com/psycarticles/2002–14078-14001.html.

Cohen, E. (1994). *Designing Groupwork: Strategies for the heterogeneous classroom* (2nd ed.). New York: Teachers College Press.

Conrad, R. (2006). "Report: School System Still Failing Black Kids," The Halifax Chronicle-Herald. Available at: http://www.herald.ns.ca/Metro/499603.html.

Crosse, S., Burr, M., Cantor, D., Hagen, C., and Hantman, I. (2002). *Wide Scope, Questionable Quality: Drug and violence prevention efforts in American schools.* Rockville, MD: Westat (in affiliation with Gottfredson Associates).

Curle, A., Freire, P., and Galtung, J. (1974). "What Can Education Contribute Towards Peace and Social Justice? Curle, Freire, Galtung Panel," in M. Haavelsrud (Ed.) *Education for Peace: Reflection and action.* Keele: University of Keele, pp. 64–97.

Davies, L. (2004). *Education and Conflict: Complexity and chaos.* London: Routledge/ Falmer.

Deng, Z. and Luke, A. (2008). "Subject Matter: Defining and Theorizing School Subjects," in F. M. Connelly, M. F. He and J. Phillion (Eds.), *The Handbook of Curriculum and Instruction.* Thousand Oaks, CA: Sage, pp. 66–87.

Dietz, M. (1989). "Context is All: Feminism and Theories of Citizenship," in J. K. B. Conway and J. Scott (Eds.), *Learning About Women.* Ann Arbor: University of Michigan Press, pp. 1–24.

Ellsworth, E. (1989). "Why Doesn't This Feel Empowering? Working Through the Repressive Myths of Critical Pedagogy," Harvard Educational Review, 59(3), 297–322.

Epp, J. R., and Watkinson, A. M. (Eds.). (1996). *Systemic Violence: How schools hurt children.* London: Falmer.

Epstein, D. and Johnson, R. (1998). *"Sexualities, Nationalities, and Schooling," in Schooling Sexualities.* Buckingham: Open University Press.

Erickson, C. and McGuire, M. (2004). "Constructing Nonviolent Cultures in Schools: The State of the Science," Children and Schools, 26(2), 102–16.

Franklin, U. (2006). "What of the Citizen?" in *The Ursula Franklin Reader: Pacifism as a Map.* Toronto: Between the Lines, pp. 87–99.

Galtung, J. (1969). "Violence, Peace, and Peace Research," Journal of Peace Research, 6(3), 167–92.

——(1996). *Peace By Peaceful Means: Peace and conflict, development, and civilization.* London: Sage Publications and International Peace Research Assn.

Garrard, W. and Lipsey, M. (2007). "Conflict Resolution Education and Antisocial Behavior in US Schools: A Meta-Analysis," Conflict Resolution Quarterly, 25(1), 9–38.

Gewertz, C. (2006). "Reactions to School Climate Vary by Students' Races," Education Week, 5 and 16.

Gilligan, C. and Brown, L. M. (1992). *Meeting at the Crossroads: Women's psychology and girls' development.* Cambridge, MA: Harvard University Press.

Gladden, R. M. (2002). "Reducing School Violence: Strengthening Student Programs and Addressing the Role of School Organizations," Review of Research in Education, 26, 263–99.

Gordon, T., Holland, J., and Lahelma, E. (2000). *Making Spaces: Citizenship and difference in schools.* London: Macmillan.

Griffin, P. and Ouellett, M. (2003). "From Silence to Safety and Beyond: Historical Trends in Addressing Lesbian, Gay, Bisexual and Transgender Issues in K-12 Schools," Equity and Excellence in Education, 36(2), 106–14.

Hahn, C. (1996). "Gender and Political Learning," Theory and Research in Social Education, 24(1), 8–45.

Harber, C. (2002). "Not Quite the Revolution: Citizenship Education in England," in M. Schweisfurth, L. Davies and C. Harber (Eds.), *Learning Democracy and Citizenship: International experiences.* Oxford: Symposium Books, pp. 225–37.

Harris, I., and Morrison, M. (2003). *Peace Education* (2nd ed.). Jefferson, NC: McFarland.

Harris, R. (2005). "Unlocking the Learning Potential in Peer Mediation: An Evaluation of Peer Mediator Modeling and Disputant Learning," Conflict Resolution Quarterly, 23(2), 141–64.

Hazler, R. and Carney, J. (2002). "Empowering Peers to Prevent Youth Violence," Journal of Humanistic Counseling, Education and Development, 41(2), 129–49.

Henry, A. (1994). "The Empty Shelf and Other Curricular Challenges of Teaching for Children of African Descent," Urban Education, 29(3), 298–319.

Heydenberk, R. and Heydenberk, W. (2005). "Increasing Meta-Cognitive Competence Through Conflict Resolution," Education and Urban Society, 37(4), 431–52.

hooks, b. (1994). *Teaching to Transgress: Education as the practice of freedom.* New York: Routledge.

Houser, N. (1996). "Negotiating Dissonance and Safety for the Common Good: Social Education in the Elementary Classroom," Theory and Research in Social Education, 24(3), 294–312.

Jones, T. (2004). "Conflict Resolution Education: The Field, the Findings, and the Future," Conflict Resolution Quarterly, 22(1–2), 233–67.

Jull, S. (2000). "Youth Violence, Schools and the Management Question: A Discussion of Zero Tolerance and Equity in Public Schooling," Canadian Journal of Educational Administration and Policy (17). Available at: www.umanitoba.ca/publications/cjeap.

Kumashiro, K. (2000). "Toward a Theory of Anti-Oppressive Education," Review of Educational Research, 70(1), 25–53.

——(2004). "Uncertain Beginnings: Learning to Teach Paradoxically," Theory Into Practice, 43(2), 111–15.

Lederach, J. P. (1995). *Preparing for Peace: Conflict transformation across cultures.* Syracuse, NY: Syracuse University Press.

Little, J. W. (1993). "Teachers' Professional Development in a Climate of Educational Reform," Educational Evaluation and Policy Analysis, 15(2), 129–51.

McIntosh, P. (2005). "Gender Perspectives on Educating for Global Citizenship," in N. Noddings (Ed.), *Educating Citizens for Global Awareness.* New York: Teachers College Press, pp. 22–39.

McNeil, L. (1986). *Contradictions of Control: School structure and school knowledge.* New York: Routledge.

Morrison, B. (2007). *Restoring Safe School Communities: A whole school response to bullying, violence and alienation.* Leichhardt, NSW, Australia: Federation Press.

Noddings, N. (1992). "Social Studies and Feminism," Theory and Research in Social Education, 20(3), 230–41.

Noguera, P. (1995). "Preventing and Producing Violence: A Critical Analysis of Responses to School Violence," Harvard Educational Review, 65(2), 189–212.

Otten, E. H. (2000). "Character Education," ERIC Digest. Available at: www.eric.ed.gov (accessed May 1, 2006).

Popkewitz, T. (1991). *A Political Sociology of Educational Reform.* New York: Teachers College Press.

Reardon, B. (1996). "Militarism and Sexism: Influences on Education for War," in R. Burns and R. Aspeslagh (Eds.), *Three Decades of Peace Education around the World: An anthology.* New York: Garland, pp. 143–60.

Robinson, K. (2005). "Reinforcing Hegemonic Masculinity Through Sexual Harassment: Issues of Identity, Power and Popularity in Secondary Schools," Gender and Education (Australia), 17(1), 19–38.

Ross, M. H. (2007). *Cultural Contestation in Ethnic Conflict.* Cambridge: Cambridge University Press.

Sadker, D. (1999). "Gender Equity: Still Knocking at the Classroom Door," Educational Leadership, 56(7), 22–6.

Salomon, G. and Nevo, B. (Eds.). (2002). *Peace Education: The concept, principles, and practices around the world.* Mahwah, NJ: Lawrence Erlbaum Associates.

Scheckner, S., Rollin, S., Kaiser-Ulrey, C., and Wagner, R. (2002). "School Violence in Children and Adolescents: A Meta-Analysis of the Effectiveness of Current Interventions," Journal of School Violence, 1(2), 5–32.

Sears, A., Clark, G. and Hughes, A. (1999). "Canadian Citizenship Education: The Pluralist Ideal and Citizenship Education for a Post-Modern State," in J. Torney-Purta, J. Schwille, and J. Amadeo (Eds.), *Civic Education Across Countries: Twenty-Four national case studies from the IEA Civic Education Project.* Amsterdam: International Association for the Evaluation of Educational Achievement, pp. 111–35.

Simon, K. (2001). *Moral Questions in the Classroom.* New Haven, CT: Yale University Press.

Skiba, R. (2000). *Violence Prevention and Conflict Resolution Curricula: What works in preventing school violence.* Bloomington: Indiana University Press.

Slee, R. (1995). "Adjusting the Aperture: Ways of Seeing Disruption in Schools," in R. Slee (Ed.), *Changing Theories and Practices of Discipline.* London: Falmer Press.

Stein, N. (1995). "Sexual Harassment in School: The Public Performance of Gendered Violence," Harvard Educational Review, 65(2), 145–62.

Stevahn, L. (2004). "Integrating Conflict Resolution Training into the Curriculum," Theory into Practice, 43(1), 50–8.

Torney-Purta, J., Lehmann, R., Oswald, H., and Schultz, W. (2001). *Citizenship and Education in 28 Countries: Civic knowledge and engagement at age 14.* Amsterdam: IEA (International Assn. for the Evaluation of Educational Achievement).

Weikel, B. (1995). "'Girlspeak' and 'Boyspeak': Gender Differences in Classroom Discussion," in J. Kleinfeld and S. Yerian (Eds.), *Gender Tales: Tensions in the schools.* New York: St. Martin's Press, pp. 7–11.

Weinstein, H. M., Freedman, S. W., and Hughson, H. (2007). "School Voices: Challenges Facing Education Systems after Identity Based Conflict," Education, Citizenship and Social Justice, 2(1), 41–71.

Williams, J. (2004). "Civil Conflict, Education, and the Work Of Schools: Twelve Propositions," Conflict Resolution Quarterly, 21(4), 471–81.

Woyshner, C. (2002). "Political History as Women's History: Toward a More Inclusive Curriculum," Theory and Research in Social Education, 30(3), 354–80.

7   Improvisation, Violence, and Peace Education

Ilan Gur-Ze'ev

Peace education is currently working hard to achieve homogeneity and ethnocentristic-oriented cohesion in the face of growing awareness of the philosophical challenges presented by post-structuralist philosophies. This awareness, however, has not yet culminated in systematic reflection on the central challenges, conceptions and aims of peace education, neither on its cultural, political and philosophical preconditions, histories and fruits. The present collection may contribute to this much needed theoretical effort. Until this very moment, however, peace education is a field of research and a celebrated practice with no serious theoretical framework/grounding (Gur-Ze'ev, 2001). Peace education has not made the slightest effort to reconstruct its history, let alone a critical history of peace education as a spiritual, educational and political effort that begins with the prophets and the Early Church ranging to various "heretic" movements and oppositions to hegemonic theology, culture, and social structures. Peace education is currently actualized and developed with no historical consciousness, neither a systematic conceptual reflection on its central values, concepts and ideals. Systematic historic and conceptual analysis of the field and its main challenges are beyond the scope of this chapter. In this chapter, I will restrict myself to a short reflection on the relations between three concepts: peace, violence and improvisation. I will try to show that the concept of improvisation might be of special relevance to any attempt to articulate and actualize counter-education which addresses the threats inflicted by present-day peace education to free, anti-dogmatic, creative and erotic humans.

In my mind, one of the shortcomings of the present hegemonic peace education as a practice, as an ideology, and as a field of academic research is the missing elaboration of relations between peace and violence, peace and metaphysical violence, peace and structural violence, peace and counter-violence, peace and power, peace and revolt, peace and defiance, peace and insubordination, and peace and passive disobedience. There are other central concepts, such as "education" and "consensus" which should be systematically analyzed in this context and this is surely solely a partial list. Any attempt to conceptualize the practice of peace education and to critically reconstruct its practices and agendas should go into the analytics, evaluation, and rethinking of these relations, concepts, and strivings that are their impetus. If violence is seriously to be questioned, it should be evaluated and addressed in face of well-classified ends. It is time to ask: what is the aim of peace education? What should we learn from the tension between the explicit aims and the unconscious and sometime wordless telos of peace education? And even more so, what is it that peace education veils, symbolizes, works for, and is a naïve agent of?

The possibility of justice as a relevant ethical framework and as a manifestation of overwhelming unjust power is not to be uncoupled from the challenge of a worthy confrontation of the presence of effective violence. Violence which enables a specific order with specific borders, limits and conditions facilitates effective silent consumption and transformed reproduction of fruitful normalization processes. These normalization dynamics produce stable virtual "illusions" concerning the "reality" of harmony, tranquility and peace. In post-modern arenas, peace is a precondition for reproducing productive self-forgetfulness, surrendering and enhancement of the "not-I" in the "I" as a loving, protected, edified human agent. Violence celebrates having the upper hand in the form of "peace" and "normality" and makes possible the invisibility of normalizing violence. This understanding calls on us to address the essence of violence and its truth. This is why it is so important to listen to Walter Benjamin when he tells us that:

> the task of a critique of violence can be summarized as that of expounding its relation to law and justice. For a cause, however effective, becomes violent, in the precise sense of the word, only when it bears on moral issues.
>
> (1978: 277)

The challenge of violence is properly addressed in relation to the truth of peace in its proper context. And the contexts vary historically and analytically. There are important differences between: (1) the context of a religious perception of a pre-redeemed world controlled by the anti-Christ; (2) the context of a revolutionary tradition that relates to a not-yet-emancipated order of things; and (3) the context of the McWorld as a post-utopian arena. Peace–violence relations in the McWorld represent the human being as it is swallowed by total immanence. This is but a partial manifestation of immanence where capitalist globalization has the upper hand and plays the role of "the absolute," traditionally reserved to God, Universal reason and the authentic "I." The McDonaldization of reality, in other words: postmodern normalizing education, realizes "peace" as an omnipotent, unchallenged, "neutral"/absolute-moral(ess) totality that organizes, represents, consumes/destroys, recycles Being in its particularities.

Faced with an ever-disenchanting-hiding position, the truth of violence, with its tempting-fascinating ends and fruits, varies according to whether it is enacted/conceived in a pre-redeemed world, at a pre-liberated historical moment, or alternatively after its realization as peaceful diverse-dynamic-hybridic-ecstatic post-modern hyper-reality. It differs dramatically when it is in the service of redemption/emancipation or, as a realization of its opposite, in the form of a conservative, imperialist, dictatorial or "Luciferian" presence, to be met with morally justified (counter-)violence. "Peace education" in such a context could be realized, according to present "post-colonialists" such as Peter McLaren, Ilan Pappe and Howard Davidson, in education for resistance and struggle for a future peaceful, harmonious, post-revolutionary reality. Totalitarian good-natured post-colonialists presently long for it in the academic ivory towers or in million-dollar roomy-tranquil apartments in prosperous suburbs. This kind of peace education in the form of education for resistance might be realized in diverse forms: from direct and open war to defiance, insubordination and disobedience of various kinds: this is a difference that makes a difference.

This line of conceptualization studies violence in relation to sharp binary dichotomies such as justifiable–unjustifiable ends. It addresses the question of requirements for defined preconditions, limits and yardsticks for maintaining power in the form of law and order of the kind that makes peace possible. Here power, as Hannah Arendt claims, is not a synonym for violence but its opposite. Power makes possible the res publica, the public dimension, peace. Violence, on the other hand, bursts out in the absence of power, so according to Arendt: "the amount of violence at the disposal of a given country may no longer be a reliable indication of that country's strength or a reliable guarantee against destruction by a substantially smaller and weaker power" (1969: 2).

However, in the first place, it is violence, effective violence, that makes possible and constitutes the stability of power; the kind of power that forms law, order and official representations of justice and lawful executions; lawful destruction or re-education of "the violent ones" who threaten "peace," "law" and "order," within which is the kind of vita activa that Arendt presents as a civil virtue.

A serious philosophical elaboration of peace education cannot be content with socio-historical reconstructions which confirm the conceptual relations between peace and violence and represent "peace" as an extreme and highly effective manifestation of violence that hides its origin and telos in the form of lawfulness, security, and peaceful normalization. If we could rest in face of such manifestations, we would have "only" to evaluate and determine the preferable violence according to the higher and more valuable aims which justify this violence on the path toward harmony, peace, or nothingness. Peace education, however, cannot be satisfied even with such a titanic mission. Its challenge is even greater, more demanding and traumatic and far more dangerous if it is to be worthy of its name and true to its responsibility.

Recognition of the intimate relations between peace, as an absence and as a reality, and (different kinds and degrees of) violence is present in the cosmogony of many cultures that have faced the challenge of Being and nothingness, existence and suffering/meaninglessness.

In the most fundamental sense, the very creation of the world, its very existence as a destruction of nothingness or the unlimited, as Being as an opposition to nothingness, is an offense against peace and justice, against the harmony within nothingness. According to Anaximandrus:

> the unlimited (apeiron) is both principle (arche) and element (stoicheion) of things that exist, being the first to introduce this name of the principle ... it is neither water nor any other of the so-called elements, but some other unlimited nature, from which all the heavens and the worlds in them come about; and the things from which is the coming into being for the things that exist are also those into which their destruction comes about, in accordance with what must be. For they give justice (dike) and reparation to one another for their offence (adikia) in accordance with the ordinance of time.
>
> (Barnes, 1982: 29)

The Gnostic tradition seriously addresses the challenge of peace and violence. It offered an alternative from its early beginnings in the first and second centuries in the Middle East to the nineteenth-century Romantics and twentieth-century philosophers, poets and political thinkers to the present new-age spiritual alternatives. Of special importance for us here is the Gnostic conception that nature and history are the embodiment or the arena of the rule of an evil God. It is the God of creation, of nature, of the body and psyche, of history; it is a wrathful God of peace-war, law, limits, productivity and history into which the human is thrown. The Other, the God of love, does exist, but is present only as an exile.

The human who is aware of his or her living on earth in Diaspora acknowledges that the triumph of the God of the Bible is, however, never complete. Diasporic life is still an open possibility—even in face of the ongoing triumph of the violence of the Evil God. This is because the exiled God is still traceable, and a leap into worthy existence is, despite all, possible in the life of the pneuma, the truly spiritual, undetermined, not-to-be-controlled human dimension. The psyche is mobilized by ethics and the body is controlled by physical law; these constitute false "peace" and adored-frightening violence that are responsible for the constitution of what Schopenhauer understood as "the Maya curtain" in human existence.

Normalized humans who are overwhelmed by effective education, physical needs, and political manipulations forget their forgetfulness and cooperate with the exile of the true God. They disregard the possibility of Gnostic knowledge and the possibility of transcending existence that is ruled by the false dichotomy between peace and violence, good and bad, law and unlawfulness. However, Pneumaticos, the spiritual human, as already the excommunicated heretic Christian Gnostic Marcion thought in the second century, might liberate himself and live beyond good and evil (von Harnack, 1990). Here moral struggles are articulated in opposition to the hegemonic traditions, and in extreme cases of this tradition "peace" or "peace education" is conceived as a manifestation of fundamental violence.

Within this framework, peace is violence. But violence, even the worthiest, does not strive for "peace" or for any other religious "home-returning" project. Any of these projects offers redemption and is necessarily reigned over by the Evil God. It is present in nature, in history and in the "body," which the pneumatic human should do his or her best to transcend in the framework of ontological Diaspora. This position with various modifications and alterations does not apply only to the first centuries in the Middle East. It is a constant challenge to Western thinking and politics to this very day. It is of special relevance for Schopenhauer, Nietzsche, Heidegger and present-day post-structuralist philosophy, to which current peace education is in debt much more than it is aware of.

Another "pre-modern" challenge to the presumptions, conceptions and goals of present-day peace education comes from another version of Diasporic philosophy, which offers an alternative view of the relations between violence and peace. This challenge understands the relations between peace and violence by totally negating the Gnostic dualistic scheme. Here too, "peace" is a manifestation of evil. Yet the Gnostic Evil God is conceived here as the true God. His kingdom, as the universe after the exile of the God of love, is for the Gnostics "the Godly city". The true believer is conceived, however, as exiled in the "earthly city":

> I distinguish two branches of mankind: one made up of those who live according to man, the other those who live according to God. I speak of these branches also allegorically as two cities, that is, two societies of human beings, of which one is predestined to reign eternally with God and the other to undergo eternal punishment with the devil. For at the very start, when the two cities began their history through birth and death, the first to be born was the citizen of this world, and only after him came the alien in this world who is a member of the city of God, one predestined by grace and chosen by grace, one by grace an alien below and by grace a citizen above.
>
> (Augustine, 1957: 415)

For St. Augustine, the preference for peace is to be decided not in a neutral way and not under any conditions. On the contrary, only under very specific conditions is "peace" desirable and a value whose realization is to be striven for as an ultimate, justifiable end: solely in the framework of true belief in the right way of the redemption of humans and the world. In this sense, this conception of peace is opposite to the one praised by most secular peace-education activists. For in their mind, earthly peace means homogeneity, harmony and human self-realization in this world as the perfect, or at least the best possible, "home." For Christian theology as represented by St. Augustine, peace, genuine peace, is only possible by transcending the "earthly city" and by dwelling in "the Godly city," its opposite.

Here St. Augustine follows the Socratic tradition and connects redemption to the possibility of transcendence as attaining the light of the true knowledge. This is one of the preconditions for the totalizing dimension of Western education and its being swallowed, reproduced, and re-presented in the service of hegemonic violence. Present peace education has lost its theological sources and its theological conceptualizations. It has also lost its humanist orientation, as well as its total commitment to the imperatives of reason and to the revolutionization of the general human condition toward its full emancipation. But it has not lost its commitment to the fundamental "home-returning" project and the kind of fear of the Apeiron, ambivalence and Life; of being situated between transcendence and immanence in eternal homelessness that cannot be calmed or appeased.

While speaking the language of moral politics, present-day peace education fails to submit non-contingent justifications for its claims, practices, and hopes for a state of peace. It cannot offer foundations, claims, and aims that transcend mere contextual violent/stable, political constructs. It fails to offer a relation of peace and violence that is self-evident, or a peace philosophy that is sacred and transcends the endless productivity/futility of mere language games.

In the present-day, postmodern condition, there is no naïve-nostalgic-grotesque room for a serious challenge to the hegemonic claim to knowledge by the totally other. Present-day reality destroys any vivid Spirit. The McWorld has no room for a new Moses, Jesus, Buddha, or Marx, nor for a new Hitler. In the present modern and pre-modern conditions, the otherness of the Other is terrorized while proclaimed as evil, or as a dangerous epistemological gift. This is a hopeful situation where there is room for love, prayer and struggle. But what room is left for hope, love and struggle in the postmodern arenas? In cyberspace, the otherness of the Other is ridiculed, presented as a grotesque or even internalized in the global pleasure machine as a mere "attractive," a "link," "site," or "item." Or an "experience that can make it for you," namely as an ornament or a plaything to be consumed for a passing moment in a context where there is no transcendence or escape from immanence, namely from meaninglessness; not even a tragic exile that incubates a worthy-redeeming waiting. Peace, how terrible, here has the upper hand.

This conception is immanently committed to totalizing information and to purging the threatening gift or "saving" humanity from its danger by all necessary means. Inseparable here are the procedures of purging the Other of his or her epistemological otherness, structural violence, and the "direct" individual and collective violence. This is the Lebensraum of a "normalizing education." One of our aims should be to unveil the relation between the success of these violences and their invisibility as a manifestation of mental health and collective stability, order, law, and "peace." Within the framework of counter-education we are called to question beyond "critique" the present order of things and its "bettering." Such dichotomies prevent counter-education, which is beyond functionalism, critique and fear of Apeiron and Life that drive Western education toward "home-returning" projects. As manifested today by Levinas, within the Diasporic alternative, peace is not an earthly stable power-relations with no effective opposition or "the return of the multiple to unity, in conformity with the Platonic or Neoplatonic idea of the one" (Levinas, 1996: 162).

However, within history, for St. Augustine it is impossible to conceive "the city of God" disconnected from "the earthly city": they are always to be envisaged in their mutual relationship. Moreover, while real peace is only to be conceived in "the city of God," its rival city strives for peace too. The division is not only, as in current peace education, between a state of peace and a state of violence (or conflict), but in parallel also between two essentially different states of peace. One might also say between two different sets of violences, one secular, the other sacred violence, namely "peace."

"The earthly city" is in constant "pursuit of victories that either cut lives short or at any rate are short-lived" (Augustine, 1957: 425). Yet as the manifestation of triumphant violence, these victories contain also goods, albeit only "the lowest kind of goods." Among these "lowest kinds of goods" attained by warfare, St. Augustine counts "earthly peace" (ibid.: 425). The point that is important for St. Augustine, which is forgotten by today's peace education, is that (earthly) peace is only attainable by warfare: "Thus to gain the lowest kind of good it covets an earthly peace, one that it seeks to attain by warfare; for if it is victorious and no one remains to resist it, there will be peace" (ibid.: 425).

According to St. Augustine, there are higher goods than earthly peace; these "belong to the city above, in which victory will be untroubled in everlasting and ultimate peace" (ibid.: 427). This other kind of peace is totally other than the peace that is tenable in the "earthly city," and it is even conditioned by transcending from the peace that the "earthly city" and its victories can offer. St. Augustine offers us two levels of analysis: on one level, he represents a Western philosophical tradition which after being secularized by Kant, Hegel, and Marx could lead to a kind of universalism within which idealists, pragmatists, and even (very) "soft" postmodernists could share peace education. In peace education, as developed by pragmatists, feminists, multiculturalists, and certainly by positivistic-oriented functionalists who strive for social stability and free, prosperous national and international markets, all trends relate to human rights and resist direct and explicit violence in the name of universal rights such as freedom from persecution or exploitation. Here the division between peace and violence is clear-cut, and the very commitment and quest for peace are left unaddressed and unproblematized.

On the second level, it is St. Augustine, more than present-day peace-education theorists and practitioners who follow his essentialism, who seriously addresses the issue of peace and problematizes the quest for peace in relation to the essence of the human and her ultimate goal. In Augustinian terms, the ideal and the reality, which peace education strives for, are the "earthly city" in its most stringent form. For St. Augustine, this is something unavoidable in this world, yet it is a challenge to overcome if redemption is to be realized.

We see St. Augustine's doctrine and the educational attitude he represents in Western thinking not solely, but part of, violent control of Western consciousness and a manifestation of epistemological violence enacted against its disciples. At the same time, however, it is worth acknowledging its dialectics and its transcendental element. It contains an antagonism to the whole order, of which "peace" as a desire, as an ideal, and as a reality, is but a part. As such, it is a constant challenge to this order, while being part of it, and it contains an important emancipatory potential. This dimension of challenging the hegemonic realm of self-evidence and the imperative to overcome philosophy and existence is surely missing from the concept of peace which functions in the various trends in current peace education.

Following St. Augustine, we claim that what in the political arena is called "peace" is one of the extreme manifestations of successful terror. Levinas sees the seed of this condition already in "Greek wisdom" and pinpoints its violent nature in which human peace is awaited on the basis of the truth:

> Peace on the basis of the truth—on the basis of the truth of knowledge where, instead of opposing itself, the diverse agrees with itself and unites; where the stranger is assimilated ... Peace on the basis of the truth, which—marvel of marvels—commands humans without forcing them or combating them, which governs them or gathers them together without enslaving them, which through discourse, can convince rather than vanquish.
>
> (Levinas, 1996: 162)

This totalizing concept of peace in its relation to true knowledge allows the effective de-humanization of humans and their formation into collectives. At its peak it makes possible and secures consciousness, which is committed to "true" solidarity. It creates and generously awards the willingness of the individual to sacrifice herself for the collective, its security, ideals, values, and horizons. As such, it is part and parcel of the violence which produces borders, wars, and Others as objects of education, destruction, redemption, and emancipation. Yet it is a concept of peace conditioned by abandonment of reflection and transcendence. It is a manifestation of one's being swallowed or constructed by the ruling realm of self-evidence. With the assistance of good parents, devoted teachers, supportive friends, beautiful texts, and endless other ways, it produces brave warriors to protect its fears and destroy its internal and external enemies. As such, it actually manifests human forgetfulness of Diasporic love. It enhances domestication; empowers tranquilization that reflects the victory of normalizing education. It is peace as "repose among beings well-placed or reposing on the underlying solidity of their substance, self-sufficient in their identity or capable of being satisfied and seeking satisfaction" (ibid.: 162).

This concept of philosophy, which was dominated by the Platonic quest for light and love of truth, is embarrassed and feels guilty in current Western thought. It finds it hard

[to] recognize itself in its millennia of fratricidal, political, and bloody struggles, of imperialism, of human hatred and exploitation, up to our century of world wars, genocides, the Holocaust, and terrorism; of unemployment, the continuing poverty of the Third World.

(ibid.: 162)

Modern peace education is very much influenced by the ideas of the Enlightenment and its visions of a future perfect world. In light of the exile of God and the overcoming of superstition, and with the power of rational critique, scientific reasoning and social progress in education, science and technology, it promises deification of humanity and eternal peace. Lessing, Kant, Condorcet, Rousseau and the false promises of the rosy future awaiting humanity after the beheading of Louis XVI are impossible to understand disconnected from the transformation of the idea of progress: from a religious teleological "home-returning" project to the secular Garden of Eden-like redemptive fulfillment. The secular "home-returning" project in the form of revolution or peace education becomes possible only by overcoming the promise of Godly redemption, but still in the framework of a "home-returning" metaphysics. In its revolutionary and educational formats, it offers human progress as the manifestation of the advance of earthly freedom, which inherits the religious metaphysical quest for transcendence and its victory over anti-Christ, Satan, or other manifestations of "the earthly city."

Franz Rosenzweig presents a very different version of an alternative to the hegemonic peace-education concept of "peace" as the antinomy of "violence." He challenges any attempt to present mundane politics as the genuine, appeasing, Garden of Eden, refusing to accept "emancipation" as the historic realization of the human potential totally to control nature, social reality, the mysterium and Fortuna. Rosenzweig goes farther than St. Augustine. He offers not just a different concept of historical progress toward peace and redemption but actually an alternative conceptual apparatus for the centrality of exile, nomadism, and Diaspora. This apparatus offers a different kind of religiosity and hospitality: the hospitality of Diasporic life; an alternative co-poiesis amid nomadism, which replaces "peace" as standstill in the form of continuity with peace as the hospitality of love of an enduring improvisation of the one who actualizes eternal creative moral responsibility every moment anew (Peretz, 2003: 17).

At the same time, however, Rosenzweig stands with St. Augustine against the Enlightenment's concept of progress and the promise of rational peace in the framework of secular history. His rejection, however, does not end up as a religious mirror-picture of humanist arrogance and violence. He presents a very different kind of Diasporic, a poiesis which becomes co-poiesis; an alternative to the secular-revolutionary and Christian-positive-redemptive Utopias alike.

He offers the position of Judaism concerning the responsibility of the Jew. According to Rosenzweig, Judaism stands detached from history, refusing to become part of the normal power-game, its rules, strives and goals. The Christian, Rosenzweig tells us, anchors his belief to the past, to the beginning of the road, to the first Christian. "Although the center is only center between beginning and end, its main stress nevertheless moves towards the beginning" (Rosenzweig, 2005: 368). Rosenzweig nevertheless emphasizes that the Christian, when true to himself, is essentially Diasporic. This is because when "he thus turns alone toward the Cross, he may forget the judgment"—but he remains on the way, in eternal Diaspora, even if on the wrong home-returning path: "the Christian consciousness, absorbed entirely in faith, pushes toward the beginning of the way, to the first Christian, to the Crucified one" (ibid.: 368.). It leads Christianity to "expansion into everything, simply into everything outside" (ibid.: 369). While Jewish consciousness, "rooting into its own innermost" (ibid.: 369), "gathered entirely in hope, toward the man of the last days, to David's royal shoot" strives toward the future (ibid.: 368). Jewish history is a separate history (ibid.: 427), the history of a relic.

> If the Messiah comes "today," the remnant is ready to receive him. Jewish history is, in defiance of all world history, history of this remnant against power as the fundamental concept of history and against All worldly history [that] is about expansion.
>
> (ibid.: 427)

The Jew is therefore essentially and not temporarily or partly a Diasporic human, witnessing universal history while always within himself. The text/universe in its wholeness is his home, for all time in the nowhere, in the in-between: dwelling as an eternal nomad between the word and its meaning (lessness), between this world and the world-to-come; he forever "awaits salvation," eternally "on the shore" (ibid.: 428) of transcendence as something "put into our blood at birth, toward the future coming of the Kingdom" (ibid.: 428).

Diasporic counter-education does not annihilate itself in the form of a belief and praxis for paving the way to the Messiah/deliverer/genuine revolution within the framework of a positive Utopia, "peace." Here messianism is true to itself by refusing any vision of a future peace, resisting any positive Utopia and any worldly, stable, appeasing "home." It insists on eternal Diaspora which negates its negation by realizing the ideal of transcendence from this world to the world-to-come: every day, every moment, is a flash-eternity of a possible change, an open gate for the appearance of The Totally Other. It is the Messianic dimension. It is present in the form of the unique day of change eternally to be waited for. As such, it is realized in facing the presence of the absence of peace as a worthy gate for the relation to the law of the Torah (ibid.: 428–29). Facing redemption as an eternal Messianic awaiting is actualized in the eternal anti-dogmatic reinterpretation of the text, rearticulating our relation to Life and the further study of the Torah which refuses any call to participate in the violence that promises "progress," redemption or "peace."

At the same time it commands responsibility and worthy addressing of any form and occasion of injustice. As in Stefan Heym's Achashverosh: The Wandering Jew (Heym, 1983), God is freedom, and the Jew is in eternal Diaspora, wandering as an eternal critic, an eternal nonconformist, an eternal responsibility for Tikun Olam, an eternal Other to any king, priest and prophet. And as such, he will never know, neither will he bring, homogeneity, consensus or "peace."

Peace education that challenges the fruits of normalizing education should challenge both the quest of totalizing homogeneity and the dogmatic quest for difference as two alternatives which within the framework of peace education pave the path for the "home-returning" self-forgetfulness. Co-poiesis and enduring responsible improvisation might offer a counter-education which will open the door to an alternative to the present peace education.

A counter-education that seriously addresses the challenge of loss, exile, and the deceiving "home-returning" projects accepts that no positive Utopia awaits us as "truth," "genuine life," "worthy struggle," "pleasure," "peace" or worthy/unavoidable self-annihilation. Loss is not to be recovered or compensated; not for the individual nor for any kind of "we." And yet, Love of Life is the home of the Diasporic in the Socratic sense of Eros as an attracting absence of the beautiful. Counter-education should invite the Diasporic to the hospitality of responsible Love of Life. Such hospitality denotes the absence of non-consensual creativity and calls for overcoming conventional morality and the other imperatives of the ethnocentric "we," its self-evidence, its normality, its counter-resistance of the oppressed and its normalized patriotic citizenship.

Response-ability and respond-ability (Gur-Ze'ev, 2005: 26) toward non-collective, toward pre-subjective and existential kinds of homelessness, toward erotic Diasporic existence, might offer new beginnings and a kind of becoming-toward-the-world (ibid.: 32) as against becoming-swallowed-by-the-matrix; an awakening. Flourishing out of Love of Life, it might make possible an awakening, which will open the gate not to "emancipation" but to transcendence from the endless various and conflicting "home-returning" projects and their complementary forms of exile/exiling, nomadism and slumber dwelling.

The determination for Diasporic life and the possibilities opened by Diasporic counter-education is always ironic. It is never at home, it is never in peace. It gives birth to something at all times immensely more important than the individuality of the Diasporic individual as in the relation of the artist to her great creation. It is creation. A symbol of Love of Life as creation that always transcends herself to the otherness of the Other as the Feminine to the Masculine and the born baby as an act of genesis, as Eros to the not-yet, as The Totally Other to the infinite not-yet fertilized potentials of each moment. The absence of "peace" is a precondition for the edification of these potentials. The absence of tranquility and of homogeneity is here of special importance and it gives honor to space, voice, sound, movement, visibility, smell, and contact. The absence of "peace" and the overcoming of the illusion of peace are the birth moment of an alternative togetherness as offered by responsible improvisation which actualizes co-poiesis. The heart of improvisation is this movement within co-poiesis (Ettinger, 2005a: 703–13) as a togetherness offered by Love of Life. As shown by Ettinger, who was instrumental in the development of this concept, it gives birth to the totally new and the wholly unexpected. The Diasporic human faces its hospitality as alterity and togetherness, not as "peace"; a form of non-instrumental playfulness that manifests erotic responsibility to Life at its best. It is an invitation which offers hospitality, the Not-Yet, not "home" but the Spirit of Diaspora that is not threatened by silence, by the absence of ethnocentristic-oriented dogma, rituals or psychic structure that is pre-organized and demands surrender and playing by the rules. It is silence that hosts here, the self-educated gaze, the eye that meets again genuine religiousness and the responsibility that is realized with, in front of, and in preparation for the participation of the Otherness of the Other as a friend, as a companion, as a worthy rival, as an unanswered question, as an indispensible manifestation of the entire cosmos and its holiness. As such, co-poiesis opens the gate to improvisation that is part of the reply and part and parcel of the most concrete, daily manifestation of the "femininity," of the birth-giving spirit of the co-poiesis, which is so different from the "masculine," instrumental "homes" and political "peace."

Diasporic counter-education is part of an improvised-courageous stance facing the dangerous waters of the river of fear, of ambivalence and rival "truths." A striving against the fear of landing on the demanding, never satisfied banks of loss. This fear is a lieutenant of "the fall" and enhances the various and conflicting "home-returning" projects that are all united in one thing only: in the promise of an end to ambivalence, alterity and Life; in the promise of an end to the Odyssey, in the promise of "peace." The togetherness that responsible improvisation offers as an alternative to "peace" is not rational/irrational in the sense established by hegemonic philosophical and political discussions, nor is it ethically justifiable in normalized paths. It is pre-rational and pre-ethical, yet it has a form; it is aesthetically "justified," allowing ethics and rational deliberation. It is also beyond "negative" and "positive" Utopia. Still, improvisation does represent hope and manifests the possibility of The Totally Other within the actualization of co-poiesis which is more fundamental than "peace" and so much more than the promise to end alterity, alienation, and suffering by returning to the peace incubated within thingness and corporiality.

Peace education is part and parcel of the hegemonic normalizing education. Such awareness is a worthy introduction of an alternative kind of togetherness, Diasporic togetherness, where improvisation as a concept, as an ideal, as a way of life is central for the possibility of counter-education. In opposition to the various agendas in present-day peace education Diasporic togetherness as actualized in the dynamics of improvisation does not call us to return "home" to sentimentalist-ethnocentric alternatives or to anti-humanist mechanical "solutions" and compensations for the loss incubated by departing from nothingness, "homeland" or "the one."

Improvisation manifests the dialectics of response-ability and respond-ability (Gur-Ze'ev, 2005: 26–7). It is not "constructive" nor is it merely "negative"; it is far from a manifestation of "resistance" to oppression or suffering and loss. Improvisation represents a creative-speculative attunement, a different kind of gaze and response-ability that makes possible responsibility that offers co-poiesis in the infinity of the moment, each moment anew. It involves a kind of intimacy with the richness of the cosmos and its inviting dynamics, impulses, drives and meaning-creation. Here hospitality enables creative compassion, where the alterity of the otherness of the Other is an unavoidable partner in creative realization of playful Love of Life that strives not back "home" but eternally toward the Not-Yet, the unknown and the never-in-peace happiness/suffering of the Other as alterity and companion.

Improvisation, when true to itself, transcends any limited context, border, dogma, regulations, drives, habits and fears—dwelling in the infinity of the moment and the ecstasies of the here and now. It is essentially dynamic, overcoming itself and the immanence that makes welcome the drive for transgression; it offers holiness each moment anew. It is a mimesis of Genesis; it dwells within the erotic unknown, attuned to the music of the not-yet gazing at the manifestations of Life, playfully responding to it in the right manner before any rational calculation and regardless of the will or direction of any colonizing power/temptation. Its acknowledged-blessed "homelessness" transcends suffering and fear into worthy suffering and responsibility as crea-tive Love of Life, a kind of "peace" that does not serve the victory of violence that has successfully silenced its victims.

Improvisation is not rhetorical, rational and ethical in the traditional Western concept of knowledge and intersubjectivity. This is why normally it is conceived as irrelevant for peace education. It offers, however, a pre-rational and pre-ethical quest for the true, the beautiful and the right in a manner that transcends Western binary subject–object, body–spirit, natural–human, human–Godly dichotomies. These separations parallel Western detachment of the aesthetic, the ethical, the intellectual, the bodily and the political—detachments that are reflected also in the saying of the psyche and in somatic silence, dichotomies which are preconditions for "peace" and "war" (and other kinds of violence). Diasporic counter-education transcends hegemonic peace education and introduces improvisation as happy playfulness that weaves anew the symbolic, the existential, the musical, and the intellec-tual creative attunement; a reply of responsible-playfulness to alterity, to suf-fering and to anti-erotic pleasures as a serious play, as co-poiesis; serious play as the wind of the wings of hope manifesting the concreteness of the presence of Love. It is more fundamental then "peace" as an a-historical moment—in a way an anti-historical and anti-peace moment. Within its never-set horizons, art becomes a form of life in a specific, material historical moment that seeks or creates bodily conduct and genuine togetherness with the cosmos in its most specific, even microscopic, manifestations in the infinity of the instant.

Improvisation is of vital importance for a kind of peace education that will not be part and parcel of normalizing education: in co-poiesis, improvisation offers a togetherness that is not pre-imposed or predicted-directed by someone or something: it is the manifestation of the spirit of freedom that meets the gate between silence and "voice," between respond-ability and response-ability; Love of Life communicates joyfully. The kind of peace it offers accepts the invitation of alterity and of the Not-Yet, creates each moment anew, without being imprisoned in any predetermined model, interest, habit, or violating threats or temptations. Only the imperative of refusing shackles and resisting any exterior limitation enlightens improvisation worthy of the name. Because it is not the fruit of subjectification processes, and since it is prior to "genuine intersubjectivity," such an overcoming of what is presently called "peace" makes possible happy, responsible nomadism. It opens the gate not to "peace" as totalizing homogeneity neither to endless meaninglessness fragmentation as a gate for postmodern salvation but to nomadism of an individual who is beyond subjectivism in the sense of "self-fulfillment." A nomad who is with herself as she is with the moment, dwelling in the cosmos in a de-territorialized and a-historical experience that is beyond her subjectivity, calculations and interests. In improvisation, she is partner to compassionate, never "peaceful," hospitality of a non-ethnocentric togetherness with the cosmos and with the Other—the Other as a homeless human who does not try to reeducate to a new "home," dogma or self-forgetfulness.

For a serious elaboration of present-day peace education it is important to note that while improvisation is uncontrolled and resists functionalist and "effective" realization, evaluation, representation and constitution, it is, at least partially, to be edified, cultivated, enhanced, improved, or at least called for. Self-constitution and self-education (which also includes much unlearning) meet here the role of teachability and learning with, for and from the partners. Here there is even room for the master as an important, serious challenge to address and overcome as part of a co-poiesis that facilitates transcendence.

Precisely because it abandons the naivety of striving for "peace" or the striving for problematic consensus of the kind Jürgen Habermas and all present-day peace education experts promise us that improvisation facilitates transcendence from the quest to return "home," back to the infinity of nothingness and to the suggestive power of "peace," "consensus," and "harmony" which are the fruits of meaninglessness. Improvisation is not a medium, not a "function," not (as so popular in today's high-tech world) an instrument that might offer big business and successful individuals "maximization of benefits," nor is it a fascinating entertainment or a reliable method for self-forgetfulness. It might become, however, a devoted agent of these and so many management experts offer today to their clients training in improvisation that will result in better management–employees relations, superior products, and higher salaries. In opposition, Diasporic Life as offered by counter-education challenges the traumatic-phallic-colonialist attitude to Life as actualized since the Socratic project and the beginning of the history of Monotheism which is nothing but the history of the search for the road to the lost "peace."

Diasporic co-poiesis offers different relations with central dimensions of Life and with central concepts and realities such as "touch," "gaze," "attunement," and response-ability/responsibility which are central to any overcoming of present-day peace education. In the form of improvisation, it furthers an attempt to re-unite or at least rearticulate the tensions, abysses, and bridges between (pre-rational) thought and action, spirit/psyche and body, "I" and the otherness of the Other in a manner that transcends traditional Western relations of space and time. It also rearticulates the relations of the bodily and spiritual touch and infinity, readdressing the relations of the moment and eternity. It facilitates that which has been so difficult for Western thought and human life since the departure from Orphic poetry and primitive nomadism: totally being in the infinity of the moment, totally dwelling in Love of Life. And it does—or does not—do so in the most concrete, embodied, deep-rooted manifestations of the de-territorialized space shared with others. That is why it is of vital relevance to exile and to nomadism of various kinds, including the collective, historical, forced exile as we know it only too well in the twentieth and the twenty-first centuries.

Improvisation is of vital importance for any counter-education that is true to itself and is courageous to face the false promises of present-day peace education by offering not emancipating negativity and ultimately eternal and comprehensive "peace" but something very different: it offers (re)birth. It brings forth responsibility, a mature, speculative ear for a gazing-at, and touching-of the newly-born in each moment anew. A de-territorialized "here" offers us, within the endlessness of improvisation, a specific, the most specific and most concrete, "here and now"; the here and now that offers not a false "home," "nirvana" or "pleasure"—it offers nomadic hospitality. A Diasporic hospitality of the co-poiesis kind. Such (re)birth is a concrete communicative creativity that has its roots in nomadic ethics (Braidotti, 2006), within the techno-scientific realities of globalizing capitalism, in the pre-rational compassion as offered by Ettinger (2005b) and the kind of togetherness that is to be educated to and trained by partners that show us/create with us new roads beyond the modern-postmodern struggle in education, assuredly beyond contextuality and the horizons of the powers that form our "self"; beyond the tradition of "critique" into the era of co-poiesis, improvisation and new forms of togetherness challenging the given reality and the presence of injustice and meaninglessness. Imagination, passion and response-ability meet here in a kind of togetherness that Unger comes very close to articulating for us:

> In the setting of our non-instrumental relations to one another, we come to terms with our unlimited mutual need and fear. This coming into terms is a search. It is a quest for freedom – for the basic freedom that

includes an assurance of being at home in the world ... The most radical freedom is the freedom to be, to be a unique person in the world as it is.

(1984: 109)

Improvisation makes possible transcendence within the triumph of the context—not to manifest the omnipotence of the immanence and homogeneity but to open the door to transcendence and heterogeneity. It calls for the transformation of respond-ability into co-response-ability, of passion into com-passion, of quasi-poiesis into co-poiesis; a kind of togetherness that does not free any of us from Diasporic existence, or from wars and the danger of self-forgetfulness, yet it opens the gate for something more fundamental than "peace": to serious playfulness with alterity in the Other and the "home-returning" quest within "our" self. It invites self-preparation and self-overcoming amidst the quest for total fragmentation and being swallowed by the immanence, on the one hand, the quest for objective, unifying "peace," on the other. It is not a "theory" neither is it a mere drive. And it is here, with us, around us, reminding us that togetherness must not culminate into oppressive collectivism and "emancipating" cruel "critiques" nor "legitimate counter-violence of the oppressed." Poiesis of the individual, of a genuine individual, opens here the door for co-poiesis, which is so much more fundamental and responsible than "peace." But the Diasporic counter-education is a path which still lacks the first step to prepare its leap. The first step toward this leap is overcoming the pre-assumptions, the passions and the telos of the hegemonic versions of present day peace-education.

References

Arendt, H. (1969). "Reflections on Violence," Special supplement, New York Review of Books, 12(4), 1–25.

Augustine, St. (1957). *The City of God Against the Pagans*. London: W. Heinemann.

Barnes, J. (Ed.). (1982). *"Anaximandrus," in The Presocratic Philosophers*. London and New York: Routledge, pp. 19–37.

Benjamin, W. (1978). *Reflections: Essays, aphorism, autobiographical writings*. New York: Harcourt Brace Jovanovich.

Braidotti, R. (2006) *Transpositions: On nomadic ethics*. Cambridge: Polity Press.

Ettinger, B. (2005a). "Copoiesis," Ephemera, 5(X), 703–13.

——(2005b). "Compassion and Com-passion," available at: http://underfire.eyebeam. org/?q=node/512.

Gur-Ze'ev, I. (2001). "Philosophy of Peace Education in a Post-Modern Era," Educational Theory, 51(3), 315–36.

——(2005). "Introduction," in I. Gur-Ze'ev (Ed.), *Critical Theory and Critical Pedagogy Today: Toward a new critical language in education*. Haifa: Faculty of Education, the University of Haifa, pp. 7–34.

——(2007). *Beyond the Modern-Postmodern Struggle in Education: Toward counter-education and enduring improvisation*. Rotterdam: Sense Publishers.

Heym, S. (1983). *Achashverosh: The wandering Jew*. Tel Aviv: Am Oved.

Levinas, I. (1996). "Peace and Proximity," in A. Peperzak, S. Critchley, and R. Bernasconi (Eds.), *Immanuel Levinas: Basic philosophical writings*. Bloomington: Indiana University Press.

Peretz, A. (2003). "The Art of Teaching and Improvisation," MA thesis, The Israeli Branch of the University of Leeds. Available at: http://www.improvcenter.co.il/texts/thesis/synopsis-english.html.

Rosenzweig, F. (2005). *The Star of Redemption*, trans. B. Galli. Madison Wisconsin: The University of Wisconsin Press.

Unger, R. (1984). *Passion: An essay on personality*. New York: The Free Press.

Von Harnack, A. (1990). *Macion: The gospel of the alien God*. Durham: Labyrinth Press.

8 Deconstructing the Other

Opening Peace

Bryan Wright

> If there is a university responsibility, it at least begins the moment when a need to hear these questions, to take them upon oneself and respond to them, imposes itself. This imperative of the response is the initial form and minimal require-ment of responsibility. One can always not respond and refuse the summons, the call to responsibility. One can even do so without necessarily keeping silent. But the structure of this call to responsibility is such—so anterior to any possible response, so independent, so dissymmetrical in its coming from the other within us—that even a nonresponse a priori assumes responsibility.
>
> (Derrida, 2004, *Eyes of the University*)

The daily conditions of a postmodern world are deeply challenging and exciting. This is particularly true in light of the contestations of ideology and tradition we witness around the world today with their impact for higher education. In the course of developing this book, Peter Trifonas and I, along with the respective scholars presented within the text, have sought to examine the deeper issues of education and peace, not as model or exemplar, but rather as an opening. An opening in the vein of the *mochlos*, or lever, identified and acknowledged in the third section of Jacques Derrida's originally published tome, *Du Droit à la Philosophie* (1990),[1] concerning the call to responsibility or performativity, of the professoriate. Derrida's image of the unconditional university, or the university to come, represents the place and space for a new discourse on peace for our time. Within the purview of the university to come, the opportunity to explore peace is opened and thereby, discovered as the opening to and for peace.

In this chapter, I look at the critical issues of peace and education within the university setting through a deconstructive lens that would strive to hold the other in fundamental alterity in the realm of the cosmopolitical, which would imag(in)e the possibility of peace through the eyes of the other. While this task seems quite daunting, and even impossible, I will endeavour to pursue the impossible as Derrida suggests, and resist any temptation to settle for a more acceptable (read easier) outcome. The task before us, as I note with the selection of the epigraph, is to answer the challenge to take up the call to peace from the arriving university to come. It is a task that will forever remain before us despite all diligence, yet we have the opportunity to engage a future that may become the present through the act of stepping through and into the opening created within the university of the future. I suggest that peace, as opening, is the opening of peace.

Engaging in this task, while daunting, seems unavoidable given the level of crises evidenced in the lives of peoples across our world and the privilege of my role as a doctoral student within the Faculty of Education. Thus, I will begin this chapter with an examination of the right to philosophy in the opening identified by Derrida's image of the unconditional university to address the role of the university in general, and the professoriate in particular, concerning peace and education. This journey will cover one of the fundamental, philosophical questions largely unaddressed within the developing field of peace education and the role of the professoriate, as it is situated within the larger discipline of peace studies within the Western academy. I will argue that through a Derridean lens crafted from the Lévinasian other, a space is opened to and for peace within the imagined unconditional university. The deconstruction of the other, in the non-space of différance, through différance, affords this opening, the opening of peace.

Deconstruction of the other must begin in the realm of a de-construction of the very process that is the unsettling of the concept. It is as much an examination of the processes of creating the concept of the other—the invention of the other—as well as it is an examination of the concept itself, the concept of the other. The nature of de-construction as Derrida states is such that it is

> inventive or it is nothing at all; it does not settle for methodical procedures, it opens up a passageway, it marches ahead and marks a trail; its writing is not only performative, it produces rules—other conventions—for a new performativities and never installs itself in the theoretical assurance of a simple opposition between performative and constative. Its *process* [démarche] involves an affirmation, this latter being linked to the coming—the *venire*—in event, advent, invention. But it can only do so by deconstructing a conceptual and institutional structure of invention that neutralizes by putting the stamp of reason on some aspect of invention, of inventive power: as if it were necessary, over and beyond a certain traditional status of invention, to reinvent the future.
>
> (Kamuf and Rottenberg, 2007: 23, emphasis in original)

In the process of invention, de-construction opens the door to the other that exceeds invention a priori. Derrida's developmental examination of the process and conceptualization of the invention of the other were presented in his Cornell and Harvard lectures of the mid-1980s, subsequently published as *Psyche: Inventions of the Other* (Kamuf and Rottenberg 2007). From this creation, or I should say, invention, the possibility unfolds a re-thinking of the concept of the other, as other, in fundamental alterity, not as any manifestation of exteriority or creation of a self/subject. Invention, Derrida states further:

> [It] is always possible, it is the invention of the possible, the *tekhne* of a human subject within an ontotheologial horizon, the invention in truth of this subject and of this horizon; it is the invention of the law, invention according to the law that confers status; invention of and according to the institutions that socialize, recognize, guarantee, legitimize; the programmed invention of programs; the invention of the same through which the other comes down to the same when its event is again reflected in the fable of a *psyché*.
>
> (ibid.: 44, emphasis in original)

Enfolded within this concept of the concept of invention lies the portal or node within the nexus of the cosmopolitical frame of our inter-subjectivity. The logos of Derridean inscription reads "the other is indeed what is not inventable, and it is therefore the only invention in the world, the only invention of the world, our invention that invents *us*" (ibid.: 45, emphasis in original). Herein the *us* is the creation of the *self*, as and in relation to the fundamental other, "for the other is always another origin of the world and *we are to be invented*. And the being of the we, and being itself. Beyond being" (ibid.: 45, emphasis in original). The opening created in the inventiveness of the other is infinitely vast and provides the essential non-space, in Derridean *différance*, to examine the linkages among philosophy, the right to philosophy, peace, and education. In this infinite space of inventiveness, which we shall never wholly traverse, I would propose the arrival (or I should say "the arrival" of our awareness) of the unconditional university that would afford the arrival of a peace as seen through the eyes of the other. But before we can be aware of the unanticipated university of the future, we must address the critical question of philosophy and the right to philosophy.

In *Eyes of the University: Right to Philosophy 2*, Derrida (2004) presents a claim that the right to philosophy must be thoughtfully guarded and ensconced within the university at large. He develops the ground for this argument through the instantiation of responsibility to the question (of philosophy itself), in the faculty of philosophy, posing "who, then, can lay claim *legitimately to philosophy*? To think, say, discuss, learn, teach, expose, present, or represent *Philosophy* [*la philosophie*]?" (Derrida 2002a: 3). Here Derrida presents the question of the question for consideration and roots it in the Faculty of Philosophy as the community of the question (ibid.: 14). It is out of, and in this fertile ground that the unconditional university springs forth. Though Derrida's speech at Columbia University was occasioned following the establishment of CIPH (*Collége International de Philosophie*) in particular, the question of the right to philosophy, its place, space, and purpose, is one that has blossomed with the aid of the winds of academic exchange and dialogue across literal and metaphorical oceans that divide.

Jacques Derrida proposed that an implicit right to philosophy exists, given the inevitable arrival and existence of international institutions such as the United Nations and UNESCO in the past century (Derrida, 2002b: 2). Further, he states that the philosophical commitment signified in membership of nation-states to these largely philosophical bodies was and is a commitment to philosophy across the global community (ibid.: 3–4).[2] In *The Right to Philosophy from the Cosmopolitical Point of View*, Derrida heralds the *democracy-to-come*, which would emerge in the unknown future and would unfold an educational system for all, committed to access to the language and culture of the people (ibid.: 3). The moral imperative to depose the hegemonies of the continental and analytical traditions of philosophical thought (ibid.: 11) could be realized through a liberation of philosophy that would "think and discern, evaluate and criticize, philosophies" (ibid.: 15) to engage an enlightened citizenry through deconstructive philosophy rather than "governmentality" (Rajan, 2007: 147).

The right to philosophy, as posed by Derrida, is built on four salient features that situate the New Humanities in the university without conditions, according to Rajan: (1) anchoring them in the habitus of knowledge; (2) free from undue influence; (3) informed by the discipline of philosophy; and (4) unconditionally ensconced within the institution (ibid.: 144–45). Rajan's reflection on the image of the unconditional university positions the New Humanities as the plane of inquiry that would encompass the multiple discourses concerning peace and thus provide the framework for the establishment of a philosophical foundation for peace education itself within the academic arena of the forthcoming university.

Specifically, this unconditional university, or university without conditions would be the place where academic freedom is coupled with "the right and freedom to question and assert, or even, going still further, the right to say publicly all that is required by research, knowledge, and thought concerning the *truth*" (Cohen, 2001: 24, emphasis in original). Even though it may seem axiomatic, it is this truth that concerns us, whereby "the university professes the truth, and that is its profession. It declares and promises an unlimited commitment to the truth" (ibid.: 24). But what are the limits on this profession, and more importantly, of the truth? To what degree have such limits been imposed upon the discourse concerning peace within the Western academy as both silence and open inquiry? I take up this question later in an examination of peace as other, suggesting that in this commitment, the university is both charged with the task and beholden to the task of truth.

Michael Peters holds the unconditional university as the place of "*freedom* to assert, to question, to profess, and to *say everything* in the manner of a literary fiction" (2004: 42, emphasis added), even to the point of critical resistance (ibid.: 43). As an unformed and potentially emergent space, the university without conditions would be true to its profession and seek to know, think, and honour the encompassing awareness of the multiplicity of all truths (ibid.: 44). Derrida lists seven propositions or theses, as the profession of the profession of the university without conditions:

1 All that is proper to men and women, framed within the constructs of Human Rights and Crimes against Humanity.
2 The history of democracy and the idea of sovereignty.
3 A responsibility to explore: (a) beyond the question of sovereignty, (b) to dissociate sovereignty and unconditionality, and (c) dissociate democracy from citizenship.
4 The history of literature, where the right to say or not say everything founds both democracy and the idea of unconditional sovereignty claimed by the university.
5 The history of the Profession/Professoriate.
6 A full examination of the "as if".
7 Questioning the very authority of the university—in the Humanities—to knowledge, to the profession (or profession of faith), and to an engaged pedagogy.(Cohen, 2001: 50–3)

In these professions that found the university without conditions, lie the opening to this emergent realm of inquiry, revealing a further fecund opening of discourse on the truths of peace from varied perspectives. Such truths of peace, or peace through the eyes of the other are nurtured and sustained within the unconditional university that would approach any question boldly and deliberately. Particularly, engaged scholars may pose fundamentally revealing questions that would examine the core ideologies that ground and sustain cultures and societies in conflict in pursuit of seeing the other. Furthermore, such inquiry would openly address all questions of peace and conflict within the broader discipline of peace studies itself as well as the field of peace education, which I address next.

Peace studies, as a discipline in the North American academy, is fundamentally adrift in the philosophical high seas of the postmodern era (Harris, 2004; Harris and Morrison, 2003; Narsee, 2005). As a postmodern project of the modern field of education, peace studies is constrained within the bounds of its narrative inside the provinciality of the academy and largely confined within field and discipline. These structural boundaries serve to limit the reach and efficacy of the young field (Wisler, 2008; Wright, 2008) both within and beyond the hallowed halls of academe, while further imposing an ontological silence upon its scholars, academics, and students in the question of peace. Consequently, peace studies will be better served through an opening of the metaphysical conversation concerning both the ontological and epistemological grounds upon which the field stands. The fundamental imperative for this conversation lies in the simple and complex conceptualization of peace: peace as opening is the opening of peace.

Peace education, then, as a sub-field of the larger discipline of peace studies, is ideally positioned within the academic arena to pose and have this meta-physical conversation that would explore the ontological and epistemological grounds upon which both the larger discipline of peace studies stands, as well as the philosophical foundations for peace education itself. However, the scope and breadth of this disciplinary work are substantially greater than what can be addressed in a single chapter, therefore, this chapter will be confined to the latter portion of this important work. Rigorous critical theoretical work can be utilized in a deliberate effort to bridge the differences of perspectives and belief structures held by scholars, academics, program founders, and administrators that are seen to separate a common mission within a singular academic field. In order to facilitate this aspect of the important work facing the field, I propose an ontological foundation built on Lévinasian and Derridean thought that allows for the opening, acknowledgment, and non-consumption of difference. On this foundation, the opportunity to build a philosophical framework for peace education rests and with it, an image of an opening of peace, or peace as the opening in peace education for the coming future.

It is the opening of peace, as concept, ethos, and pedagogy through, in, and by the fashioning of discursive forms that creates the opportunity to lay a solid foundation for the field.[3] As I have previously stated, the opening created in the moment of the arrival of the other is the space in which peace enters. This concept is built on the secularist meta-ethics of Lévinas and the incisive philosophy of Derrida as an opportunity to overcome the option of refusal (of the other) in that specific moment. Additionally, the role of the Lévinasian face in its diachronous balance of the self and other within and in the face of the face of the other represents a further possible opening of an amorphic or indeterminate lens through which to focus on the moment and its image. In the arrival of the third, the diachrony of the self and other is exposed as insufficient and requiring a response beyond ethics that would acknowledge the infinitude of the other in fundamental otherness, alterity, or infinity (Lévinas, 1969: 51). Such acknowledgment is offered in the notion of dis-interest (Gaston, 2005: 20) that compels adjudication (Manning, 2002: 155), which I draw upon to explore the opening of peace education in order to help better situate the field within the discipline of peace studies and to offer a philosophical ground for the development of its ontological foundation.

Lévinas' teleological project throughout his life may be intuited and received as the development of a secular ethics based on the self, other, and the third, or other others (Moyn, 2005: 182), but it has been revealed to be more than that in some posthumous analyses (Farley, 2005; Manning, 2002; Moyn, 2005; Thomas, 2004). Robert John Sheffler Manning's (2002) inspirational text Beyond Ethics to Justice Through Lévinas and Derrida: The Legacy of Lévinas suggests that the later works impel and compel an engaged response that receives the other in full alterity and calls forth justice through a reflection on justice beyond the face to face relation between subject and other and into the relation of multiple others, into the realm where my obligation to the singular one is crossed by my obligations to other others ... [through] the process of deliberation and adjudication between various interests that is the work of justice [which] only arises through the appearance of the third.

(ibid.: 150)

Manning meticulously examines the discourse of Lévinas and Derrida, as well as the discourse that developed between these two prominent twentieth-century philosophers and he clearly identifies the distilled essence as the opening of ethics into justice. Manning further interprets Derrida's contribution advancing the Lévinasian proscriptive responsibility into the realm of adjudication, claiming

the obligation to the singular is crossed by other obligations to other others. This situation wherein conflicting and competing obligations meet and oppose one another demands adjudication. One must consider the multiple and conflicting obligations and adjudicate between them.

(ibid.: 155)

When Manning states that Derrida exceeds the limits of ethical concerns as he enters the tendentious realm of politics and justice (ibid.: 156), the opening of ethics as framed within the worldview is exposed to its own fragile nature of judgment and the subsequent process of adjudication. It is in this opening of ethics to justice by Lévinas and Derrida that we catch a glimpse of light through a possible opening into peace, and thereby, an opening for peace and for peace education within the academic arena.

As we see in Manning's excellent exegetical rendering of these two French philosophers' search for justice, the self is challenged at the moment of the arrival of the third to exceed the limits of interest bound in singularity, or as Lévinas himself stated in his first significant text, *Totality and Infinity*, "*The other qua other is the Other*" (Lévinas, 1969: 71, emphasis in original). But we see in Lévinas' (2000) re-imaging of justice later in *Otherwise Than Being or Beyond Essence*, his maturing conceptualization of justice that only arrives in the presencing of the third (Manning, 2002: 117). Here Lévinas reflects a deliberate apositionality that mediates any distance—proximity—between the self and the third. In his own words, Lévinas' says "my responsibility for the other is troubled and becomes a problem" (Lévinas, 2000: 157), compelling me to shift my focus, or to become dis-interested in the self and more interested in the other in the face of the other other. Manning explicates this notion as "my responsibility for my other becomes a problem when it has to be measured and balanced against my responsibility for the third and by the other's responsibilities to the third" (2002: 117–18).

Elizabeth Thomas (2004) offers cogent insight and further develops the key question of responsibility, or responsibilities to and for the other/third in *Ethics, Justice, and the Human Beyond Being*. Her published dissertation, cited here, interprets this opening of ethics inside the diachronous balance of the *self* and *other* as "the face who breaks through the form of its *own appearance as a third* firstly demands justice of the 'I' who awakens to the injustice of the system" (ibid.: 106, emphasis added). It is this moment of opening within (of the *self* to the inner-*third*) that can afford the opening without, between the self and the third. The initial opening, or the opening to the self as inner third, is a necessary condition for the opening of the second, and as such, illustrates the notion of dis-interest in the *self* for a preference (or interest) in the *third*, which can obviate the refusal of the other, whether other arrives in the presence of the self, other or the third. Thomas' further exegesis of *Totality and Infinity* holds the notion of social totality as the encompassing of the self and other, along with the third. She proffers

> that justice is a moment of the ordination of subjectivity by the Other for the social totality. This is a move from the anonymity of the totality ... to the moment of singular identity before the Other, who does not justify me but demands a response. In other words, the Other does not just command/order me but commands me to command, which is to locate myself there before the Other and thus introduce myself to the whole of humanity. *Nothing remains between two. The ethical exigency must be translated into an ontological act of calculation and judgment.*
>
> (ibid.: 118, emphasis added)[4]

It is this specific moment, or act, that is the deliberative moment of adjudication in Manning (see above). Such an ontological act cannot be otherwise since one must have a prior reference position in order to act, which indeed arises from an ontological framework, whether it is acknowledged or not. The act of calculation and judgment thus serves as a relational tool to position the *self*, or subject, where such positioning is a referent to one's ontology.

Likewise, as in Manning, awakening initiates the moment of dis-interest for Thomas, or a diminishment of one's interest in/for the self in preference for the other/third, which is a concept explored subsequently throughout our discourse, or remapping of the notion of refusal. Furthermore, she understands social justice within the social totality as a rethinking of ethics and justice, which

> is not merely a rethinking of the grounds of social justice but a questioning of the meaning of the traditional grounds or foundations of justice as a presupposed, impartial universal. Thus Lévinas' claim that he did not make a distinction between the right before the other and the right before the third does not mean that he did not recognize a difference between 'ethical justice' and 'justice' as a moment of calculation but rather that

the call to justice by the Other is *already a call to respond* and make a judgement in the face of an incomparable uniqueness.

(ibid.: 118–19, emphasis added)

This call is more than a request put to the self; it arrives in the form of a demand that requires action. Any action in the opening of the self to the third is a shift in the proportionality of interest between each party. Moreover, this shift—or interest—is the very act of interest, or the between being that may be more commonly understood as inter-subjectivity.[5]

Thomas enframes the metaphysical concern of ethics and justice within the opening of ethics to justice as

the two-side event of the face to face encounter itself that it is a relation that confronts the unique other but also concerns itself with the whole of humanity. Thus while, for Lévinas, the ethical relation is linked integrally to justice, it is of utmost importance that the one is not reduced to the other.

(ibid.: 116)

Her interpretation of this moment in Lévinasian meta-ethics recognizes the ontological framework that becomes inescapable despite Lévinas' disavowal of ontology itself. Our interest in the opening of the moment lies in the scope of interest—the whole of humanity. It is specifically the breadth of the scope of interest, or the whole of humanity that evokes the notion of peace through a privileging of interest in all others in relation to the self. Such a notion is captured by Manning thus,

according to Lévinas the relation between the self and the other not only produces knowledge of the Other, but that which is much more important than mere knowledge and which calls such knowledge into question: the self's obligation to and responsibility for the Other. The relation between self and other produces this obligation and responsibility and thereby also produces the idea of justice, nonviolence and peace. The relation subjects the subject to this obligation and this responsibility. In other words, it remakes the subject [or the *self*] as a responsible subject, an ethical subject, and does so even against the subject's will.

(Manning, 2002: 148)

In this moment, the moment of Lévinas' critique of a presumption of a knowledge of the other, Manning is not claiming that such a knowledge is full, or complete, or a consumption of the other; rather, he is suggesting that mere knowledge becomes the opening to obligation and responsibility for the other.

This metaphysical act invoking justice serves as the impetus for a further shift in the lives of the self, others, and the third. The opening now becomes the avenue for a movement from refusal of the other (upon her/his arrival to the self) to the embrace of all others, and in this embrace one may discover the seeds of peace. Such an embrace of all others as compelled by justice, subordinates judgment to justice in order to preclude differential responses arising from adjudication that would produce injury to the other. Furthermore, this embrace may be understood as an act of hospitality without reservation.

Jacques Derrida's œuvre makes a significant contribution beyond Lévinasian secularist ethics in his promulgation of unconditional hospitality. Hospitality as a concept remains a crucial element to relationship and community. This concept as an extension of the same ontology presented earlier in this chapter provides another key block in the foundation of metaphysics for the field of peace education within the academy. Pure hospitality "consists in welcoming whoever arrives before imposing any conditions on him, before knowing and asking anything at all" (Derrida, 2005: 7). Derrida claims "the question of hospitality is thus also *the question of the question*; but by the same token the question of the subject and the name as hypothesis of descent" (2000b: 29, emphasis added). In this moment of Derridean philosophy, we see the weight of the subject in the moment of arrival precisely as the given of the given that constitutes subjectivity. He poses to the subject—*self*, an irrefutable and perpetual responsibility to the other in inescapable social relationality.

Certainly our asking to whom do I owe sanctuary presents many other pertinent questions as well, of which some have been already addressed. Initially, we must imagine a distinction of the stranger/other (or the other/ third) that approaches us in place—or, our abode (ibid.: 14). The stranger/ other presents his or herself unexpectedly and expects your hospitality as an irrefutable right of the stranger. Subsequently, upon receiving the other, at that very instant, the right to hospitality is diminished and transformed into the knowing of the other (Derrida, 2000a: 8). At this moment of transformation the third becomes other and demands the subject/self (see Thomas above), answer all future arrivals of the other. In this implicit demand, the unconditionality of our reception of all others is made manifest. Hospitality, due all others, is seen as a cosmopolitan right, not sentimental and not given to moral concern (ibid.: 3). Derrida goes on to explicate further that the absolute arrival of the other is the penultimate question facing humanity (Derrida, 2000b: 35).[6]

In the absolute arrival of the *other*, the question of our response is unequivocal. We must respond. But will we offer, graciously, without pretense, expectation, or constraint, our hospitality; or, shall we withdraw and seek to protect our "place"? It follows that this is the original question of peace. Now the question of peace, according to Derrida (2000a) is such that "peace implies within its concept of peace the promise of eternity. Otherwise it is not peace ... the very structure of the concept of peace, which implies a promise of indefinite, and therefore eternal renewal" (ibid.: 6). The eternity implied within peace refers to the very ontology represented in human sociality. Eternity would represent the eternal renewal to the *face of the face* of the *other* as a constant demand. Here Derrida emphatically states that for peace to be peace, for peace to mean peace, for peace to exist, it must be an expression of receptivity to the third without reservation, or hesitation. If peace is not eternal, it is not peace because as such, peace would only be a conditional relationship of privilege between the subject/self and the third. Peace invokes eternity in its demand for relationality that is not subordinated to any self or other, while presenting itself as the unknown.

Just as it is impossible to know that which is hospitality, we may infer the same for peace. However, we can do the difficult work around conceptualizing these critical questions in the space of an informed, and enlightened university, given the privilege of the right to philosophy. In *Du Droit à la Philosophie*, Derrida closes the case for an absolute right to develop and question all that is, can be thought, and considered knowledge. He sees this right as funda-mental to the development and maintenance of a critical theoretical founda-tion in higher education, and as such, the essential defense against the usurpation of the academy and its quintessential role in society. The challenge for the university in general, and peace education in particular, is to name this barrier—the reticence of academics and the academy to examine peace as the arrival of the third—and to recognize it for such. Peace thus, as the arrival of the third, is the peace that means peace to and for the other others. Certainly, the difficulty of naming this reticence may lie in the fundamental challenge posed to the very onto-epistemology of the Western academy, and as such has been frequently silenced. But this need not be the case if faculty, students, and staff of each 'discipline' can be open to the arrival of the third that would disrupt the status quo and develop a full awareness of the presencing of the *other* in unconditional hospitality.

Furthermore, peace education as a young, and perhaps precocious field has the opportunity to confront the refusal of peace within the provinciality of the university and answer the demand of peace at its metaphorical door. Like Derrida, I would suggest that the field of peace education engage this onto-epistemological challenge and strive for the impossible (Derrida, 2000a). We must overcome our inhibitions around peace and its demands on us to allow for its arrival within our selves, our relations to all others, and more specifically here, within the academic arena and the field of peace education.

My project in this chapter has been to build upon the metaphysical foun-dation of Lévinasian and Derridean ontology a framework that could open the doors to the possibility of an exploration of the question of peace as peace. Peter Trifonas (2003), in *Pedagogies of Difference: Rethinking Education for Social Justice*, illuminates another key step along the path of creating such a framework by drawing on the trace of critical theory in critical pedagogies to examine social change and its import for curriculum. Trifonas explicates and augments Derrida's approach to the questions of social justice and peace in his promulgation of a post-critical theoretical lens that is "an ethical opening of the subject toward the difference of the Other" (ibid.: 228). Through the creation of a new perspective for a post-critical pedagogy, Trifonas opens the discourse to a consideration "that is beyond the cognitive limits of the tele-ological trajectory of the subject of metaphysics" (ibid.: 231) into the ethical future of fundamental alterity. It is this future that will animate and inform the future of peace education in its fullness.

Peace education could embrace the difference of the other and the third, overcoming its own inertia and onto-epistemological refusal within the pro-vinciality of the university, and, thereby, expand its capacity, scope, and legitimacy within the hallowed halls of academe. Peace education could dis-cover its ontological voice in full multivocality through an investment in the development of many of the philosophical lenses presented herein. We have the basic tools to accomplish this task as well as the knowledge to produce different, more specialized implements for our challenging work. Some of the lenses have already been fashioned and only need to be honed to reveal the image, while others await discovery. The responsibility of this work lies squarely on the shoulders of the professoriate as an open engagement with *différance* in the nexus of the cosmopolitical frame of our inter-subjectivity, as we have been pointedly reminded:

> We live in a world where the foundation of a new law [*droit*]—in parti-cular a new university law—is necessary. To call it *necessary* is to say in this case *at one and the same time* that one has to take responsibility for it, a new kind of responsibility, that this foundation is already well on the way, and irresistibly so, beyond any representation, any conscious-ness, any acts of individual subjects or corporate bodies, beyond any interfaculty or interdepartmental limits, beyond the limits between the institution and the political places of its inscription.

Notes

1 Jacques Derrida's *Du droit à la philosophie* (Right to Philosophy) was translated and subsequently printed as two separate texts, with the first being *Who's Afraid of Philosophy?* and the latter *Eyes of the University: Right to Philosophy 2*. I will be referencing the second book primarily unless otherwise noted.
2 As other known scholars have understood, Derrida did not and would not use the term "global community," but I choose to use it here to frame the aggregation of the overwhelming majority of nations. Moreover, I think his reticence to have used the word "community," largely based on a disinclination to diminish difference is overcome by the number of signatories to such international charters and conven-tions, notwithstanding the repugnant attitude of non-signatories.
3 I will be drawing on Anderson's conceptualization of peace as absence of violence to any aspect of life (or being) as a comprehensive concept, which refers to general well-being (1985: 6).
4 Thomas is asserting an explicit ontological function in the face and arrival of the *other*, which contrasts with Lévinas' claim refuting ontological bias or structure. In doing so, Thomas has advanced the original work and been true to its purpose by pushing Lévinas beyond himself. This is a substantial contribution that impacts the field of peace education, and consequently, peace.

5 Etymology is a crucial lens in philosophic discourse and it is especially important to Derridean thought. The etymology of the word "interest" is derived from *inter-*"between" + *esse* "to be." It is "to concern, make a difference, be of importance." Online Etymology Dictionary. Retrieved April 28, 2008 from:http://www.etymonline.com/index.php?search=interest&searchmode=none.

6 Derrida clearly understands the fundamental right of hospitality as inviolable and consequently, interprets this right as the premise upon which he furthered the Lévinasian meta-ethic inside the frame of ontology.

References

Anderson, G. (1985). "Competing Views of Human Nature in the Politics of Peace: Integrating ideas of Cobb, Galtung, Gewirth, and Tillich," Dissertation Abstracts International, 47(02), 560. (UMI No. 8607818).

Cohen, T. (Ed.). (2001). *Jacques Derrida and the Humanities: A Critical Reader*. Cambridge: Cambridge University Press.

Derrida, J. (1990). *Du Droit à la Philosophie*. Paris: Galilée.

——(2000a). "Hospitality," Angelaki: The Journal of the Theoretical Humanities, 5(3): 3–18.

——(2000b). *Of Hospitality: Anne Dufourmantelle Invites Jacques Derrida to Respond*, trans. R. Bowlby. Stanford, CA: Stanford University Press.

——(2002a). *Who's Afraid of Philosophy? Right to Philosophy I*. Stanford, CA: Stanford University Press.

——. (2002b). "The Right to Philosophy from the Cosmopolitical Point of View (the Example of an International Institution)," in *Ethics, Institutions, and the Right to Philosophy*, trans. Peter Pericles Trifonas. Lanham, MD: Rowman & Littlefield Publishers, Inc.

——. (2004). *Eyes of the University: Right to Philosophy 2*. Stanford, CA: Stanford University Press.

——(2005). "The Principle of Hospitality 1. Interview," trans. Ashley Thompson, Parallax, 11(1): 6–9.

Farley, L. (2005). "History, Ethics and Education: Learning from Freud and Lévinas," unpublished PhD diss., University of Toronto.

Gaston, S. (2005). *Derrida and Disinterest*. New York: Continuum.

Harris, I. (2004). "Peace Education Theory," Journal of Peace Education, 1(1): 5–20.

Harris, I. and Morrison, M. (2003). *Peace Education* (2nd ed.). Jefferson, NC: McFarland & Company, Inc.

Kamuf, P. and Rottenberg, E. (Eds.). (2007). *Psyche: Inventions of the Other, Vol. I*, trans. Peggy Kamuf. Stanford, CA: Stanford University Press.

Lévinas, E. (1969). *Totality and Infinity: An essay on exteriority*. Pittsburgh, PA: Duquesne University Press.

——(1974/2000). *Otherwise Than Being or Beyond Essence*, originally published in Autrement qu'être ou au-delà l'essence, trans. A. Lingis. Dordrecht: Martinus Nijhoff.

Manning, R. J. S. (2002). *Beyond Ethics to Justice through Lévinas and Derrida: The legacy of Lévinas*. Quincy, IL: Franciscan Press.

Moyn, S. (2005). *Origins of the Other: Emmanuel Lévinas between revelation and ethics*. Ithaca, NY: Cornell University Press.

Narsee, S. (2005). "Navigating Unchartered Waters: Peace within hearts, hands and minds," Higher Education Policy, 18(4): 341–51.

Peters, M. (2004). "The University and the New Humanities: Professing with Derrida," Arts & Humanities in Higher Education, 3(1): 41–57.

Rajan, T. (2007). "Derrida, Foucault, and the University,"Mosaic, 40(2): 133–50.

Thomas, E. (2004). *Emmanuel Lévinas: Ethics, justice and the human beyond being.* New York: Routledge.

Trifonas, P. (Ed.). (2003). *Pedagogies of Difference: Rethinking education for social justice.* New York: Routledge Falmer.

Wisler, A. (2008). "Peace Knowledge: An inquiry in Post-Yugoslav higher education." PhD diss., Columbia University, New York.

Wright, B. (2008). *Educating for Cultures of Peace within the Academy: A holistic approach to peace studies in the university for the new millennium.* Saarbrücken: VDM Verlag Dr. Müller.

The (Im)possibility of Trying for Reconciliation and Peace

The Significance of Conflict, Limits, and Exclusions in Transitional Democracy

Mario Di Paolantonio

> Conflict, division, and instability, ... do not ruin the democratic public sphere; they are the conditions of its existence. The threat arises with efforts to supersede conflict, for the public sphere remains democratic only insofar as its exclusions are taken into account and open to contestation.
>
> (Rosalyn Deutsche, 1996)

Various thinkers of transitional democracy have attempted to justify trials for past state-sanctioned abuses by pointing to their ability to pedagogically show-case the principles and benefits of deliberation.[1] Such trials are thought to stage a public forum where post-conflict disagreements can peacefully be conciliated through an "educative dialogue" sustained by the consensual regulative principles inherent in court procedures. In this chapter, I argue that an interpretative model that seeks to justify and understand such trials by emphasizing the effects of an "educative dialogue," that strives for social unanimity and peaceful settlements, risks overlooking the formative pedagogical role that conflict plays in a new democracy. While not wanting to downplay the obvious significance and necessity of striving toward peaceful engagements in a transitional period, it becomes critical, amid often facile and abstract endorsements of reconciliatory forums and processes, to recover the political limits and conflicts at work in those aspirations to reconcile, to render amiable, and to juridically settle what remains unsettled. Moving beyond the attempt to dissolve conflict through dialogue and reconciliation will thus allow us to elucidate the remains that remain beyond reconciliation. It is this appreciation of the limits and of what remains beyond settlement—the contestation of forces, relations of force, and differences of force whose conflict cannot ground power firmly and finally in any one place—that proves vital for a democracy.

In what follows I unravel the above concerns by critically engaging with the conceptual shortcomings found in the work of Mark Osiel and Carlos Nino, two legal thinkers who respectively develop a deliberative pedagogical proposal from their reading of the 1985 Trial of the Military in Argentina.[2] Given that their interpretation draws on certain philosophical assumptions regarding the way in which democracy and education are linked through deliberation,

I begin with a gloss on how this link is generally conceived. I then examine how deliberation is envisioned by "transitional scholars" who concern themselves with the educative role that criminal trials play in peacefully and legitimately helping to establish a new democracy. Following my reading of Osiel and Nino's claims, I utilize "radical democracy" theory to offer another reading of the Trial of the Military, one that necessitates a more dynamic sense of the pedagogical and can account for the formative role of conflict and exclusions in reproducing and sustaining democratic subjectivity.

DRAWING THE LINK BETWEEN DELIBERATION AND EDUCATION

Both democratic deliberation and education are thought to provide an index and entry to the other through their social and interactive dimension. They are mutually presented as a process of communication and joint participation through which the discovery and reconstruction of a common task are undertaken. Various thinkers such as Amy Gutmann and Dennis Thompson (2002), Benjamin Levin (1998), and Stephen Macedo (2000) believe that at the core of both deliberation and education we find an emphasis upon a shared social experience, one that supposes that people can change and grow in understanding through the active and amicable exchange of ideas.

The dynamic process of participants shaping and transforming their position on an issue through deliberation and collective learning sharply contrasts with the prevalent "aggregative model" of defining democracy. In this model, individual interests are aggregated through the mechanisms of strategizing, coalition building, and voting, consequently rendering democracy—as C.B. Macpherson critically describes—into merely a means of registering "the desires of people as they are, not to contribute to what they might be or might wish to be."[3] Stripped of its dialogical dimension, democracy is thought to simply become a market mechanism: voters are consumers and politicians are entrepreneurs. In considering only how an already constituted interest group matches or instrumentally directs itself towards a desired policy direction, the aggregative model is unable to account for how interests and preferences are pedagogically formed and often re-formed through dialogue and the cordial sharing of public aspirations.

By highlighting the educative-dialogical dimension, it is thought that we can bring into focus the ways in which those who are likely to be affected by an outcome gather to discuss, shape, and possibly expose themselves to learning something beyond their initial position. This affords greater democratic legitimacy than the aggregate model, since there is an obvious legitimacy from joint decisions that emerge from an open and inclusive deliberative process that not only encourages one to express one's opinions but also obliges one to rethink and rework them so that they are publicly defensible and intelligible. Learning interpersonal skills of discussion, negotiation, understanding, and respect for opposing views becomes critical for deliberation to be, not only effective, but also fully legitimate as a public discourse in a democracy. Thus, democratic education often aims to foster in learners the capabilities and dispositions to partake in such deliberations.

Deliberative democrats thus appreciate that public institutions—such as schools, but not just schools – are influential sites that function to reproduce social life in overlapping networks and civic associations that extend beyond the confines of the market place and family. Our ability to deliberate as socially uninhibited and equal citizens can be fostered through public institutions that allow us to encounter how our own positions are not uniquely reasonable or without social effects. Facing contrasting ideas and having to rationally justify our positions amid public forums consequently nurtures in us a means of living with others in mutual (rational) respect, thus helping forge a peaceful civic-space.

In the next section, I trace the utilization of these ideas through another register, namely, through an interdisciplinary field that considers how trials for past abuses enact an educative deliberative forum.

EDUCATION, DELIBERATION, AND LEGAL TRANSITIONAL STUDIES

The field of "transitional studies" concerns itself with the complex process of shifting from an authoritarian rule to a democratic one. A conglomeration of political thinkers and social legal theorists in this field have grappled with the social educative role that criminal trials play in societies reckoning with the abuses of a prior regime.[4] Their approach assumes and incorporates a number of the same assumptions regarding deliberation and education glossed above. According to these scholars, we can discern certain pedagogical outcomes from trials dealing with past abuses. For instance, not only can such trials teach and cultivate a shared historical narrative of the past, but they can also provide (or so it is thought) a pedagogical occasion for recognizing and commemorating victims of past violence. Moreover, such trials are thought to stage a communicative process for building and securing solidarity around the deliberative and institutional virtues of liberal democracy. It is thought that the very form and procedures structuring the trial itself, the way in which each party comports itself and tells their story through the rules and procedural norms of the court, reiterate and help to inculcate the liberal democratic virtues of toleration, reciprocity, and civil respect. While there might be failures and compromises of law in such pedagogical trials, the important point, according to this reading, is to pay attention to the ways in which such trials foster collective memories, experiences, and normative shifts that help peacefully bind a society together in the extraordinary period of a transition.

We are clearly dealing with a different analytical appreciation of the law's role than what is conventionally understood. For suggesting that the law is responsive to extraordinary times, or that it pedagogically participates in cultivating normative shifts, profoundly stretches the commonly understood significance of the law as a measure of order and stability that stands independently from societal influences. Admittedly, then, there can be no simple compatibility between the rule of law (as an insurer of settled norms) and such pedagogical trials, which are part of the vast social endeavor to transform and re-legitimate previously defunct institutions and norms (Teitel, 2000: 11).

How are we to understand, then, the role of law in societies undergoing transitions, during a time when a society cannot properly claim the law as an established ground, or as an insurer of continuity or settled norms? The suggestion, implicitly at work in this literature, is to understand the showcasing of law during a transition as a performative or pedagogical instance that draws on the symbolic sense of the rule of law, rather than on its actuality. In other words, there is an appreciation here that, in a transitional society where institutions have to re-ground their legitimacy after periods of social upheaval, the rule of law is called upon as a performative proposition, as a necessary fictional precedent that helps to stabilize and authorize the normative shifts underway during such times. Invoking the rule of law as an exemplar—that is, invoking it symbolically pedagogically during such an exceptional period—paradoxically ensures both a measure of continuity (through the appeal to a non-arbitrary set of legal norms) and yet at the same time helps to facilitate normative change (ibid.: 223). The law is thought to play an explicitly theatrical pedagogical role here, lending its symbols and rituals of legitimate measured change to the uncertainty gripping the transition period, and in so doing teaching us about the rule of law.

This is perhaps one of the more productive points implicit in the work of those who underscore the pedagogical dimension of law, since it opens up messy questions around the symbolic, contingent, and performative educative role that law needs to play when, apparently, there are no established foundations or precedents. Rendering these issues explicit can conceivably make us sensitive to the contradictions, tensions, and inevitable exclusions underlying the need to establish a new order and forge operative norms during such an exceptional moment. However, where the analysis becomes problematic is when such trials are thought to provide an exemplary educative model that can teach us how to cordially deliberate about the divisive past so that we can enter into an "edifying conversation" with normally unwilling participants.

Drawing largely from the example of the 1985 Trial of the Military in Argentina, the respective work of Mark Osiel and the late legal philosopher Carlos Nino offer perhaps the most exemplary and sustained analyses of this position. While Nino and Osiel share many of the same assumptions about the pedagogical effects of such trials, they differ in emphasis as to the role that the "substantive" dimension plays in the deliberative process. For Nino, the Trial of the Military stages a formal conciliatory dialogue that can guide historical interpretation and public understanding in such a way that a "collective consciousness" around the "truth" and the "public good" can be derived (Nino, 1996: 147, 132–33). Whereas Nino emphasizes the way in which the public dialogue inspired by the Trial teaches a rational moral consensus to the divisive events of the past, Osiel, for his part, brackets such assumptions. Instead, he claims to focus on how the formal procedures of the Trial enable and guide an educative dialogue between exemplary adversaries so that "even the deepest disagreements are channelled into a single conceptual framework, providing common terms" but not necessarily a consensus on the good (Osiel, 1997: 49). Rather than garner a sense of solidarity forged around certain core values that may be uncovered through the Trial, Osiel forefronts a solidarity that ensues from commonly adhering to rules on how to proceed with a civil discussion of deeply divisive issues. Writing about his differences with Nino's interpretations of the Trial of the Military in Argentina, Osiel tells us that:

> The solidarity that I anticipate (and observed there) in contrast, presumes no such agreement, but merely civil engagement in disagreements by way of procedures entailing display of respect for one's adversary, respect that may be entirely procedural (and a matter of rule following) at the outset.
>
> (ibid.: 48)

Whether it is for the loftier goal of forging a "collective consciousness," as Nino would have it, or whether it is simply to initiate, as Osiel concedes, those procedural norms structuring the public engagements of former adversaries, both interpretations esteem the pedagogical model of dialogue (utilized by the trial) as the means of overcoming conflict and securing a peaceful ground for democracy amidst the precarious state of transition. For these thinkers the model of dialogue extracted by the trial becomes the means of learning to translate conflict into "disagreement," into a matter of misunderstanding that can be peacefully reconciled. This is ultimately a hermeneutical lesson, one that seeks to overcome and settle the social disruption or dissensus at play back into the folds of mutual understanding. The significance of disagreement, for both Nino and Osiel, thus lies in how it draws out different positions so that they may modify and act on each other, setting in motion a process where conflicting presuppositions can be gradually worked out and settled. According to Osiel,

> although often unpleasant and divisive in many ways, the [disagreement encountered through dialogue] creates a kind of joint understanding: that we have both faced the issues dividing us, that we are united in caring deeply about them and about what the other thinks of them.
>
> (ibid.: 43)

The trial envisioned as a hermeneutical theatre is thought to provide a forum where various groups can agree to submit their contrasting memories and allegiances to the mediation of a shared normative order that establishes mechanisms to dialogue and solve eventual conflicts peacefully, consequently helping to consolidate the new social order.

Inasmuch as this public process depends on working through contrasting memories of the past wrongs, such trials, according to Osiel, become secular rituals of commemoration, a collective site for remembering and cordially learning about the past (ibid.: 6). However, whereas conventional commemorative activities often invoke memories of social trauma through an overly affective structure of identity that tends to be celebratory and divisive, trials for administrative massacre, which place emphasis on the deliberative dialogic process for organizing memory, provide a more tempered, dialogically educative means of reaching broader solidarity and reconciling social strife.

What can be so problematic with this reading? Do we not have a type of agonistic educative democratic forum here? That is, do we not have here a means of teaching and learning how to render the "enemy" into an "adversary," into someone who can, through common rules, if not a set of minimal core values, sit down with us and engage us through their differing terms?

READING THE LIMITS: RECOVERING THE POLITICAL

The seemingly benign emphasis on dialogue offered by both Nino and Osiel needs to be critiqued on various levels, lest we miss the specificity of the political. Hence, at one level, we need to take issue with their under-theorized claim that such trials can redirect memory, with all its messy affects and identifications, away from the realm of contestation towards the realm of orderly deliberation and cordial settlements. Their rendering of memory into a "safe and proper object" through deliberation cannot account for those instances of excess, those other dejected ways of (non)speaking that, in their very incapacity to enter into an "edifying dialogue," signal what cannot be settled through deliberation, what must be otherwise remembered beyond this forum, and what remains irruptive and disruptive of the present settlements. At another level, which I unravel below, we need to account for how the educative-dialogical model that they celebrate and claim to have observed in Argentina, actually provides little or no context, consequently abstracting the specificity of the event and foreclosing any appreciation of the constitutive role that conflict plays with the turn to democracy. To better situate this critique, I need to gloss over the rather complicated legacy of the Trial of the Military in Argentina.

With the turn to democracy in Argentina, a legal process was set in motion in order to publicly account for the dictatorship's repressive strategy of disappearances. Although responsibility for the disappearances was spread widely throughout the ranks, the 1985 Trial of the Military was intended, by the government of Raúl Alfonsín, as an exemplary educative trial limited to the most senior level of the military. However, public resolve for more trials grew as it was seen to be an effective means of marking and gaining answers to the fate of those disappeared, answers which the military was not willing to divulge voluntarily. Faced with an increasing number of trials against a military that was once again closing ranks and publicly making gestures to derail the turn to democracy, Alfonsín legislated a series of amnesty laws (respectively the Punto Final law and the Obediencia Debida law) that sought to contain further prosecutions. In 1990, in the name of reconciliation, the convictions and precedent established by the Trial of the Military were further eroded and overturned through a set of pardons issued by Alfonsín's successor Carlos Menem.

It is revealing that Nino's and Osiel's readings provide no sustained analysis of how the amnesty laws, which sought to contain further trials, refract and impact on the actual legacy of the Trial. Their work makes no attempt to access the type of lesson that could be garnered from a trial whose precedent and justification for further prosecutions were actively eroded and overturned by the state in the name of social peace and reconciliation. What could it mean to reconcile public disagreements through dialogue in a context where the state actively works to close down the demand for law? Who specifically desires to dialogue and learn how to overcome differences under these terms? What are the effects of mobilizing discourses and aspirations invoking peaceful settlement under these circumstances?

Both thinkers leave these issues unspecified and unexplicated. The model of amicable dialogue that they extract from the Trial thus remains an abstraction—a pure form—that never references the historical context. While the model of dialogue that they invoke entails its own intrinsic normativity for learning how to overcome conflict, it stops short of understanding the crucial feature of dialogue "as a situated practice, one implicated by the particulars of who, when, where, and how the dialogue takes place" (Burbules, 2000: 261). Without an appreciation of the specificity of dialogue, a problematic relativization ensues, collapsing the distinct ways in which various subjects are affected and positioned by the closing down of further trials. The invitation to settle disagreements through dialogue, especially in the transitional context, is never a simple or neutral matter. For it is never purely a momentary engagement between two or more reasonable people who just misunderstand each other. Rather, it is a discursive relation situated against the background of previous relations, which are not simply matters of rational choice (ibid.).

In truth, there is something rather odd about the desire to extract an exemplary educative-model of dialogue from the 1985 Trial. Osiel claims that the Trial "enabled a discussion to occur that would otherwise never take place" between "parties that would otherwise refuse to sit down together" (1997: 49). While certainly there was an "orderly sequence of exchanges" structured through the Trial's procedural norms, a "discussion," let alone an exemplary one as Osiel envisions it, never really took place. For a cordial discussion, where those affected by an outcome gather to discuss, give shape, and possibly expose themselves to learning something beyond their initial position, seems unlikely to ensue in the adversarial setting between defendants and prosecution. In a courtroom setting such a discussion would appear rather thin, if not impossible, given the constraints and consistency in which parties must state their case through norms of argumentation designed to satisfy the law and not the terms of an edifying educative encounter.

Nevertheless, Osiel insists that courtroom deliberation is capable of staging a mutual dialogue where, "through this process, we can learn to overcome dangerous misconceptions about the other" (1997: 42). But this ignores how in fact the defense of the Junta leaders, and their supporters beyond the courtroom persistently refused to revise or modify their position regarding the so-called, "enemies of the nation." Believing that they, the naturally appointed "guardians of the nation," fought a "righteous Christian war" against "the evil of communism," they often maintained that they were ultimately not answerable to the "secular and arbitrary" laws of the new democracy.[5] The adamant refusal by the military to enter into any dialogue during the trial that could revise their position was a strategic politics played out as a means of realigning the internal consent within the ranks that was initially lost during the end of military rule and transition to democracy. In holding steadfast to their claim to being the true "guardians and saviours of the nation," who were now being unjustly discredited through this trial, the military was able to reconstitute their identity and close ranks, overcoming the many internal divisions that followed the transition. This re-forged unity—ironically drawn from an aspect of the military's defense during the trial—began to present serious threats to democracy as the government at the time became ever more compliant to the military's demand to put an end to further trials against the military, eventually enacting various amnesty laws towards that end.

In this context, what is to be gained by proposing that a trial is a useful way to begin a discussion with an initially unwilling adversary? What exactly is socially edifying about a discussion between perpetrators and victims? Nino and Osiel never address these issues, for a simple equivalence between the participants is presumed in their pedagogical model of peaceful dialogue. Given the reassertion of the military in politics, and the appeasement of the military by the state with its amnesty laws, we can appreciate that many sectors in civil society, committed to democratic politics, obviously did not aspire to dialogue so that everyone could learn "to acknowledge the differing views of their fellows." For the sake of forging democratic politics there are very good reasons not to enter into dialogue here. At an obvious level, there was no point in fashioning a dialogue with those who, through intimidation and through claims of fulfilling the "true will" of the nation, sought to foreclose all competing terms. Drawing from "radical-democracy" theory, specifically the work of Chantal Mouffe (2000), a more important analytical point to note is that, for democratic groups the incommensurable position (enacted between themselves and the military) needs to be maintained precisely as an incommensurable point, since it provides, a constitutive demarcation that is vital for defining and holding steadfast to the democratic imaginary at this crucial juncture. In other words, the re-articulation of the incommensurability between an "authoritarian imaginary" and a "democratic imaginary" allows the values of democracy—the very terms and promises that legitimized the transition in the first place—to be critically brought to the fore at a time when the state is seen to be betraying and compromising the turn to democracy. The re-articulation of the values and commitments to democracy in this way can provide the grounds to resist the politics of reconciliation; that is, the amnesty laws compromising the principles of the democratic transition.

The emphasis on dialogue, deliberation, peaceful settlement and reconciliation ends up missing the significant formative role that conflict plays in the transitional moment. For this is a moment when, in order to effect the turn to a new possibility, it becomes crucial to publicly out certain values as being incommensurable and in conflict with democratic values. Clearly there is politics of demarcation, a process of expunging and re-forging, which needs to be operative during a transition. For marking a distinction between the abject and the object of our goals and commitments is obviously constitutive of the very possibility of a transition.

This account perhaps has striking implications for understanding the pedagogical reproduction of democratic subjectivity, since it emphasizes limits and exclusions as opposed to oft-celebrated claims for an all-embracing inclusiveness. To envision democratic subjectivity as something that can be learned and forged through the inclusive norms of deliberation, elides the necessary demarcations, refusals, affects, the very politics involved in reproducing any subject position. It is thus imperative to draw out how the reproduction of democratic subjectivity is subject to particular, albeit provisional, limits (Laclau, 1996: 52–3). Rendering the limits explicit not only avoids spinning into relativism, but also makes clear that there is inevitably a politics of inclusion and exclusion at work in forging any identity or social order. Once we appreciate this, we are in a better position to face the political problem of how to keep a particular democratic order from closing in on itself, from rendering unjust exclusions. For although limits are constitutive and formative, this does not mean that they should not be questioned or challenged. In other words, explicitly acknowledging the limits of a particular demos implies accounting for its inevitable exclusions. Whether these exclusions are justifiable or not, these very exclusions nevertheless provide an outside point (a remainder) from which to question and interrupt the immanence (the self-enclosure) of any social order and its political terms.

Operating on the cusp of an emerging order, the deliberation envisioned by Nino and Osiel aims to educate and render the "good citizen" whose competence and conscience are to be attuned to the liberal virtues required for peaceful conciliation. My emphasis on conflict, limits, and exclusions is an attempt, not only to recover the specificity elided by deliberation, but also, importantly, to recover a more dynamic sense of the pedagogical than the deliberative model offers. By pedagogical, I do not mean a process whereby we learn how to settle issues by applying appropriate rules or terms for understanding, but rather a reflexive encounter with the limits. This implies a double encounter with the inside and the outside of our terms, a pedagogy of the limits where learning is forged through handling the residue or point of exclusion which can reveal or reactivate the contingency of our demos. More specifically, the pedagogical is invoked here as an encounter: (1) where we endeavor to learn about the operative limits which define us; and (2) whereby learning to ask after what remains or has been excluded, we come to better appreciate the indelible closures and exclusions upon which our political judgments and commitments are based. This pedagogy of the limits, this double gesture to read our terms, can help us to appreciate how the moment of closure, while necessary for defining and identifying democratic subjectivity, is ultimately contingent and open to contestation.

Claude Lefort tells us that the originality of democracy is the institution of the empty place of power, an opening where society can project its conflicts, and tests its various inclusions and exclusions.[6] Democracy can be well served by a pedagogy, a reflexive encounter, that can make us attentive to the limits, since democracy needs to guarantee that nobody can occupy or pretend to incarnate the empty place of power, and that any such pretensions can be publicly contested by that which is excluded. While different political forces might aim to cover over the traces of power and exclusion that they effect by invoking rhetorically powerful terms such as reconciliation and peace, a pedagogy of the limits can teach us how to read the demarcations of a particular position so that it becomes publicly visible and its inclusions/exclusions can enter the terrain of contestation. Learning to be attentive to the politics of the limits can help correct interpretative models that elide the particularities of an issue through mobilizing all-inclusive claims and reconciled solutions. It can also allow us to be more attuned to the contingency structuring any social order, to the contestations over what remains, to what is excluded through any settlement or claim to identity. This has particular resonance in societies, like Argentina, where justice still remains to be done, where the remains remain unburied and unaccounted for, where the terms of the past remain divisive and thus inherently irruptive and interruptive of any present settlement.

APRÈS COUP

Extracting from the 1985 Trial an "educative dialogue" that can be utilized as a model for forging reconciliation and peaceful settlements at best rings hollow amidst the context of post-trial Argentina where there is an active contest for defining normative space. The emphasis on the civility of rules that shelters disagreements in the foil of a cordial dialogue overlooks the necessarily contested domain of public engagements that the—monological rather than dialogical—amnesty laws and pardons inaugurated. While agreeing with both Nino and Osiel that the 1985 Trial of the Military deposits a residual pedagogical possibility in a society attempting to re-democratize itself, my emphasis and understanding of the political instantiation of democracy in Argentina are otherwise. Given the highly contested politics that an environment of state concessions, amnesty laws and pardons generates, it is critical to appreciate the tension between forces, the dimension of antagonism unleashed across society as a result of the amnesty laws and pardons. Holding steadfast to the neutrality of the dialogical model for explaining the post-trial public reactions would end up generating an apologia for the state strategy of reconciliation, falling into what Jacques Derrida describes as a discourse of "the successful foundation of the state," which produces after the fact [après coup]

> what it was destined in advance to produce, namely, proper interpretative models to read in return, to give sense, necessity and above all legitimacy to the violence that has produced, among others, the interpretative model in question, that is, the discourse of its self-legitimation.
>
> (Derrida, 2002: 270)

With Derrida's point in mind, the dialogical interpretative model that I have criticized above reveals something more than merely a benign unrealizable aspiration to overcome divisive conflicts facing a transitional society. This interpretative model—like the strategy of reconciliation wielded by the state—mobilizes a politics of sedimentation and self-legitimation that seeks to cover over the force of its decision: to cover over, as it were, how the terms of reconciliation inevitably create contestation and irreconcilable remainders that can rival and reveal its limits. In other words, by claiming to dissolve conflict through a pedagogical dialogue that gradually organizes itself around unanimity, the dialogical model elides the force and limits at work in its own persuasion to settle and conciliate a particular understanding and parsing of politics. A pedagogy of the limits is not so much a solution, or even a fully fledged proposal to counter the dialogical interpretative model, it is rather an approach, a hope for an other heading for maintaining and expanding a constant vigilance for what remains for us to think, for a way of reading and recovering the political after the fact (amid the remains) of politics.

ACKNOWLEDGMENTS

A shorter version of this chapter was originally presented at a General Session of the 62nd Annual Meeting of the Philosophy of Education Society (April 21–24, 2006), Puerto Vallarta, Mexico, and subsequently published in the Philosophy of Education Yearbook, 2007.

Notes

1 Eric Posner provides dimensions of transitional (political) trials. See, in particular, "Pedagogical Trials" (2005: 61–70).
2 I discuss Mark Osiel, Mass Atrocity, Collective Memory, and the Law (1997) and Carlos Santiago Nino, Radical Evil on Trial (1996).
3 Cited in Levin (1998: 58).
4 See Posner, "Political Trials" (2005: 61–70); also Mario Di Paolantonio, "Tracking the Demand for Legal Recall: The Foreclosing and Promise of Law in Transitional Argentina" (2004: 351–75).
5 See Frank Graziano (1992: 226). Contrary to the deliberative ideal proposed by Osiel and others, there was no mutual dialogue or respect demonstrated during the trial. Not only did the defense for the military put forth an argument that denied any implication or responsibility for human rights violations, but survivor testimonies (those who survived torture, rape, mutilation, at the hands of military during its "dirty war"), were discredited by the defense as part of international conspiracy; "the defence referred to prosecution witnesses as losers of the armed battle who were now retaliating in an insidious unarmed campaign on the 'psychological front', 'conquering hearts and minds' through the trial's publicity." Graziano (1992: 51).
6 See Claude Lefort, Democracy and Political Theory (1988: 17). Also see Claude Lefort, "Inventar la democracia: entrevista con Claude Lefort" (1997: 617–27).

References

Burbules, Nicholas C. (2000). "The Limits of Dialogue as a Critical Pedagogy," in Peter P. Trifonas (Ed.), *Revolutionary Pedagogies: Cultural Politics, Instituting Education and the Discourse of Theory*. New York: Routledge, p. 261.

Derrida, Jacques (2002). "The Force of Law: The 'Mystical Foundation of Authority'," in Gil Anidjar (Ed.), *Acts of Religion*. New York: Routledge, p. 270.

Deutsche, Rosalyn (1996). "Agoraphobia," in R. Deutsche, *Evictions, Spatial Patterns and Public Art*. Chicago: Graham Foundation for Advanced Studies in Fine Arts, pp. 269–327.

Di Paolantonio, Mario (2004). "Tracking the Demand for Legal Recall: The Foreclosing and Promise of Law in Transitional Argentina," Social & Legal Studies, 13(3), 351–75.

Graziano, Frank (1992). *Divine Violence*. San Francisco: Westview Press.

Gutmann, Amy and Thompson, Dennis (2002). "Deliberative Democracy Beyond Process," Journal of Political Philosophy, 10(2), 153–74.

Laclau, Ernesto (1996). *Emancipation(s)*. London: Verso.

Lefort, Claude (1988) *Democracy and Political Theory*. Minneapolis: University of Minnesota.

——(1997). "Inventar la democracia: entrevista con Claude Lefort," Metapolitica, 1(4), 617–27.

Levin, Benjamin (1998). "The Exceptional Requirement for Democracy," Curriculum Inquiry, 28(1), 57–79.

Macedo, Stephen (2000). *Diversity and Distrust: Civic education in a multicultural democracy*. Cambridge, MA: Harvard University Press.

Mouffe, Chantal (2000). *The Democratic Paradox*. New York: Verso.

Nino, Carlos Santiago (1996). *Radical Evil on Trial*. New Haven, CT: Yale University Press.

Osiel, Mark (1997). *Mass Atrocity, Collective Memory, and the Law*. London: Transaction.

Posner, Eric (2005). "Pedagogical Trials," in "Political Trials in Domestic and International Law," Chicago Public Law & Legal Theory Working Paper 87, 61–70.

Teitel, Ruti (2000). *Transitional Justice*. New York: Oxford University Press.

Index